CONSTITUTIONAL
SOUND BITES

CONSTITUTIONAL SOUND BITES

DAVID J. SHESTOKAS

CONSTITUTIONALLY SPEAKING
Lemont, IL

Questions? Comments?
CONSTITUTION@SHESTOKAS.COM
© 2015 David J. Shestokas, J.D.
All Rights Reserved
Published by Constitutionally Speaking
Lemont, IL

ISBN 978-0-9969281-1-3

About this Book

The *Constitutional Sound Bites* series was originally published in three English language volumes as Kindle books on Amazon. That series was collected, reorganized and translated into Spanish as *Cápsulas Informativas Constitucionales* in collaboration with Dr. Berta Arias. The Spanish language edition was the first of its kind, and contained new material not available in the English Kindle series. This edition now mirrors the Spanish edition to enable readers to share our American constitutional heritage in either language.

Upon completion of the Spanish edition, this English edition was created as a complement. Together, the Spanish and English editions facilitate discussion among friends, family and students in order to share and understand important concepts about America, overcoming the problems that sometimes occur with different levels of language ability.

Within this book the three volume format is maintained. The reason for this is that the focus of each volume is different. Those differences are explained in the introduction to each volume.

While the material is organized into subject areas, the reader can open to any page, read a particular entry and gain knowledge about how a specific provision or idea of the Declaration of Independence, Constitution or Bill of Rights fits in with the goals of America's Founding: to create a limited government that protects the liberty and freedom of its people.

The book's overall goal is to raise awareness that the Founding Documents and Principles of America are not liberal or conservative, Republican or Democrat, but are the heritage that bind its people together into a community known as America.

This Book and the Men on the Covers

The original English version was published in three volumes, each with its own cover. Each cover featured a Founding Father related to the volume's content, and these covers are now included in the combined book.

Since these covers have appeared the question has been asked: What are they listening to? *Constitutional Sound Bites* grew out of the author's experience with radio. The men in the headphones are listening to their audience.

George Washington is listening to questions regarding the conduct of the Revolutionary War, arguments for and against his becoming king, and the direction of the country.

James Madison is listening to questions about the Constitution's ratification process of 1787–89, *The Federalist Papers* and the need for and content of a Bill of Rights.

Benjamin Franklin is listening to an international audience befitting his world renown as a scientist, his status as America's first Ambassador to France and his experience as America's first advice columnist. Franklin would have been the perfect twenty-first century talk show host.

Thomas Jefferson is listening to deep questions such as: How are all men created equal? What is the pursuit of happiness? While one can imagine Jefferson entertaining questions in a studio, he would likely have found his home as a blogger.

Constitutional Sound Bites is devoted to explaining ideas and principles communicated and acted upon by America's Founders. There is limited biographical material regarding particular founders. What follows is a brief background of the men on the covers.

Given the chance, what questions might you ask of these men?

George Washington:
Father of the Country

George Washington is known as the Father of the Country. He was Commander and Chief of the Continental Army. The army he led defeated Great Britain, then the world's super power, in the War for Independence. At the end of the war in 1783, at a time when great generals often were crowned kings, Washington left public life, showing the world that there would be no royalty in the new America.

In 1787 he was recruited to serve as President of the Philadelphia Convention that created the Constitution. His signature is the first on the Constitution. Two years later, in 1789, he was elected first president under the new Constitution. In 1797, he set a precedent that would last over 140 years by retiring after eight years.

Washington, by example, demonstrated the idea that in a republic, there was to be no royalty and that government worked best for the people when citizens served and returned to private life.

James Madison:
Father of the Constitution and the Bill of Rights

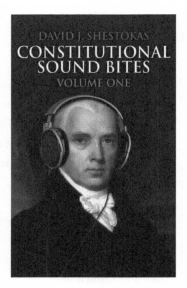

James Madison is known as the Father of the Constitution and the Bill of Rights. In May, 1787, Madison arrived at the Philadelphia Convention with the most detailed plan of government of any delegate. It was called the Virginia Plan, and contained most of the principles that are now found in the Constitution.

He had spent months preparing for the convention by studying governments from ancient Rome to eighteenth century England. Madison also kept the best record of the Constitutional Convention debates. He was author of twenty-six of the Federalist Papers that explained the Constitution in 1787–88.

In 1789, he authored the amendments that would become the Bill of Rights. From 1809–17 he served as fourth President of the United States.

Benjamin Franklin:

Printer, Scientist, Diplomat

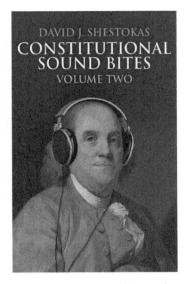

Benjamin Franklin holds the distinction of being the only man to sign all three documents that freed the colonies from England and established the United States as an independent nation: The Declaration of Independence, The Treaty of Paris and The Constitution.

He was a printer and writer of books and newspapers in Pennsylvania. He was world famous for his inventions, among them the lightning rod, bifocal eyeglasses, and the Franklin stove. He was the first United States Ambassador to France and secured French support for the American Revolution, a critical factor in defeating the British.

He was the oldest delegate to the 1787 Constitutional Convention at eighty-one. His speech at the end of the convention showed him to be the most optimistic.

George Washington's chair at the Constitutional Convention had a half revealed sun carved in the seat back. When the Convention had finished drafting the Constitution, Franklin said of the chair: *"I have often looked at that sun behind the president without being able to tell*

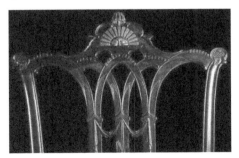

whether it was rising or setting. But now I . . . know that it is a rising . . . sun."

Thomas Jefferson:
Author of the Declaration of Independence

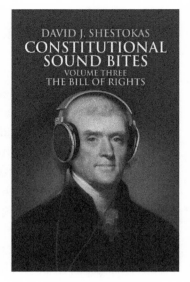

Thomas Jefferson was the author of the Declaration of Independence and the Statute of Virginia for Religious Freedom, third president of the United States, and the founder of the University of Virginia. He was only thirty-three years old when the Declaration of Independence gave voice to the aspirations of a new America. Jefferson was an attorney and employed that training in his writing.

Following Benjamin Franklin, he was America's second ambassador to France. He was serving in France in 1787 and did not attend the Philadelphia Convention. During his time as president from 1801 to 1809 he was responsible for the Louisiana Purchase, which doubled the size of the United States and expanded the country westward from the Mississippi River to the Pacific Ocean.

Contents

About this Book . . . . *vii*
This Book and the Men on the Covers . . . . *viii*
Prologue 1

Volume One
Introduction, Volume One 7
Constitutional Considerations 9
Thoughts on the Declaration of Independence 17
The Constitution's Preamble 21
Article I: The Congress 27
Article II: The President 33
Article III: The Supreme Court 39
Article IV: Government Relations 43

Volume Two
Introduction, Volume Two 49
Constitutional Considerations, Volume Two 55
Thoughts on the Declaration of Independence, Volume Two . . . 59
Article I: The Congress, Volume Two 65
Article II: The President, Volume Two 71
Article III: The Judiciary Volume Two 75
Article IV: Government Relations, Volume Two 79
Article V: Amendments 81
Article VI: Debts, Oaths and the Supremacy Clause. 87
Article VII: Ratification 91
The Bill of Rights, Volume Two 95

Volume Three
Introduction, Volume Three 103
Constitutional Considerations 107
Thoughts on the Declaration of Independence 111
The Bill of Rights, Volume Three 113
The First Amendment 117
The Second Amendment: The Right to Bear Arms 127

The Third Amendment: No Quartering of Soldiers 131
The Fourth Amendment 135
The Fifth Amendment: The Right to Remain Silent
   and Four More 141
The Sixth Amendment: Right to Counsel and Five More 147
The Seventh Amendment: Right to Jury in Federal Civil Cases . .155
The Eighth Amendment: Ban on Cruel and Unusual
   Punishment 159
The Ninth Amendment: Protection for Unenumerated Rights . .163
The Tenth Amendment: Powers Reserved to the People
   and the States 167

Epilogue 171

A Note from the Author 173

About David J. Shestokas 177
About Berta Isabel Arias 179

Acknowledgements 181

Notes About *Cápsulas Informativas Constitucionales* 183

The Declaration of Independence 185
The Constitution of the United States of America 191
Amendments to the Constitution of the United States
   of America 205

Selected Bibliography .215

Prologue

On September 17, 1787, the Constitutional Convention finished its work and sent the proposed Constitution out to the states for approval. Within a single day, 500 English language copies of the proposed Constitution were printed for distribution to elected officials around the country.

Pennsylvania Orders Copies of the Constitution

Travel and communication were slow in the eighteenth century, but Philadelphia was the capital of Pennsylvania, and Pennsylvania's legislature was the first to receive the new Constitution. Within a week the Pennsylvania legislators ordered 4,500 copies for their citizens. Three thousand copies were ordered in English and 1,500 ordered in German.

In 1681, immigrants from Germany's Rhineland area founded Germantown, Pennsylvania. They had left their homes primarily because of ongoing wars between Germany and France. By 1787 one in three citizens of Pennsylvania spoke only German. Approval of the new Constitution by German speaking Pennsylvanians was just as important as the approval of the English speakers.

The Pennsylvania legislators knew it was crucial that the German speaking citizens received information about the plan for a new government in their native language. The Constitution was to be based upon the consent of the governed and a person could not consent to something he could not understand. The translated Constitutions were mandated by the principles of America's Founding.

Pennsylvania would not be the only place that language would be important in the story of the Constitution.

New York Considers its Dutch Speaking Community
In 1624, New Amsterdam became the capital of the North American colony of New Netherland. Though New Amsterdam was captured by the English in 1664 and renamed New York in 1665, over one hundred years later a significant Dutch speaking community still lived in New York. In 1787 New York, care was taken to ensure widespread distribution of a Dutch translation of the proposed Constitution. The Constitution's approval by the Dutch speakers of New York was thought as important as approval by the English speakers.

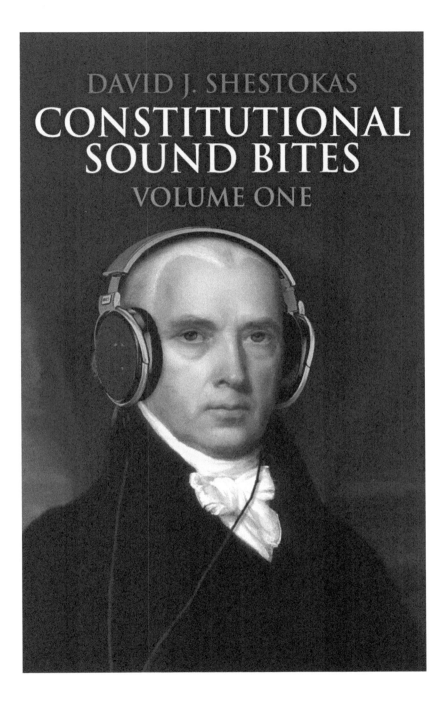

DAVID J. SHESTOKAS

CONSTITUTIONAL SOUND BITES

VOLUME ONE

DEDICATED TO ALL WHO HAVE MADE SACRIFICES THAT
AMERICA MIGHT BE FREE, AND MY GRANDMOTHER,
BARBARA SHESTOKAS, WHO CAME FROM LITHUANIA
IN SEARCH OF FREEDOM AND SHARED HER LOVE
OF AMERICA WITH EVERYONE SHE TOUCHED.

CONSTITUTIONAL SOUND BITES

VOLUME ONE

DAVID J. SHESTOKAS

CONSTITUTIONALLY SPEAKING
Lemont, IL

Introduction, Volume One

In the twenty-first century, we've become used to getting information in small doses of media, *sound bites*, short blog posts and 140 character Tweets. Modern leaders, understanding mass media, beginning with Franklin Roosevelt, ("A date which will live in infamy . . ."), through Barack Obama ("I don't want to pit Red America against Blue America . . .") have turned this into an art form. They understand the communications of the day.

The leaders of Revolutionary America understood the communications of their day. After the proposed Constitution was completed on September 17, 1787 the battle for ratification began. Much of it took place in the mass media of the eighteenth century: newspapers. Long essays appeared around the country.

The most famous of these essays was a series that became known as *The Federalist Papers*. These eighty-five articles by John Jay, Alexander Hamilton and James Madison when collected result in a book of about 400 pages. While *The Federalist Papers* (and the newspaper essays written by opponents of the Constitution) remain good reading, it's not the way Americans get information in the twenty-first century.

If Jay, Hamilton and Madison had been trying to reach modern Americans, they would have changed their techniques and shortened their messages to accommodate modern communications, perhaps into one minute ideas. This book contains one minute ideas or "sound bites" about America's Founding and The United States Constitution.

The Constitution can be an intimidating and complex subject, but like most complex matters, it becomes clear when presented in pieces. As host of the weekly radio show Constitutionally Speaking, I discuss the constitution and its relevance to our lives in "small pieces." In addition to the weekly program I do a daily one minute radio presentation entitled *"A Minute of Constitutionally Speaking."* The "minutes" vary between stories of the people involved in America's founding, the philosophy behind the founding documents, and the institutions created by the Constitution. This book is the first of a series containing "sound bites" about a document that is neither Republican nor Democrat, not liberal or conservative, but American.

The Founding of a Nation on Ideas

In 1787 the American experiment in self-government was in danger. The country had been founded just eleven years earlier based on ideas that had never before served as principles to guide a nation. In 1776 The Declaration of Independence summarized these ideas. The principles revolved around beliefs in the inalienable* rights of the individual, the equality of all men before the law and that the only legitimate government has the consent of the people being governed. In 1787, the first effort to put those principles into practice, the Articles of Confederation, was not working well.

The failings of the Articles of Confederation led the movers and shakers of the day to revise the organization of the United States. The result was the Constitution. The Preamble set forth the Constitution's goal: *"to secure the blessings of liberty for ourselves and our posterity."*

Our forefathers constructed the Constitution so many years ago with the fervent desire to secure our liberty. Today, that goal is scrutinized, challenged, and under fire daily. The responsibility to protect the hard won liberty now rests with you and me. An understanding and appreciation of the Constitution's relevance to our lives is a giant step in protecting our liberty and that of our children.

Thomas Jefferson was once asked about the point of the Declaration of Independence. His short answer was that he was trying to explain the "common sense of the subject." That's what *Constitutional Sound Bites* attempts to do.

---

* The question is often asked, "Is the word in the Declaration of Independence *unalienable* or is it *inalienable*?"

The final version of the Declaration uses the word "unalienable." Some earlier drafts used the word "inalienable," which is the term modern dictionaries prefer. The two words mean precisely the same thing.

This book uses "inalienable" unless quoting the Declaration.

Constitutional Considerations

**What events during the Christmas of 1776 saved United States
independence and set the stage for the Constitution?**

In the fall of 1776 the British drove General George Washington and the
Continental Army out of New York. Only 3,000 of the original 20,000
American troops escaped by retreating across New Jersey and into
Pennsylvania. By late December the soldiers were cold, starving, and
many were ill with cholera, small pox or dysentery.

With Washington's Army in retreat, Congress fled Philadelphia for
Baltimore, Maryland. The American cause appeared to be lost.

On Christmas Day, snow swirled as a winter storm brewed. In the
dark of night the soldiers were ordered to board boats that had been
commandeered up and down the Delaware River. They were setting
out to cross the river, made treacherous by high winds and large ice
floes. They were heading back east into New Jersey. As the soldiers
prepared, General Washington ordered Thomas Paine's words of inspiration from *The American Crisis* read to his troops. Paine's essay
began: "*These are the times that try men's souls.*"

After the harrowing river crossing and a ten hour march through
the frigid night, the Continental Army attacked the enemy in Trenton,

NJ. The Americans were victorious. Without that bold winter attack that ended with a desperately needed victory, there likely would never have been a United States Constitution.

How long after the Declaration of Independence did the Constitution go into effect?

The government established by the Constitution began operating March 4, 1789, nearly thirteen years after Independence had been declared.

The United States declared independence on July 4, 1776. Beginning in 1777 the country was organized under the Articles of Confederation. The central government under the Articles was weak with little authority to raise revenue. Amendments to the Articles required the unanimous consent of the thirteen States and such unity was rarely achieved. This combination handicapped the new country with a lack of revenue and a government often unable to act.

In May of 1787, the Confederation Congress authorized a convention to propose amendments to the Articles of Confederation. On September 17, 1787, instead of amendments, the delegates presented an entirely new Constitution. September 17th is now observed in the United States as Constitution Day. The proposed Constitution was presented to the Confederation Congress and sent to the States for ratification later that year.

Why does the United States have three branches of government?

Through history if a single person made the law, enforced the law and judged the law, there was no law, only the opinion of that person. The Framers believed that separating making law (legislative) from enforcing law (executive) and interpreting the law (judicial) would best protect the freedom of all. This is why there are three branches of government.

The American Constitution was the first effort in world history to separate government functions between legislative, executive and judicial branches. The Framers viewed this division of power as fundamental to protecting freedom and liberty while establishing a country.

The thoughts leading to the American government's structure can be traced over 1800 years to ancient Rome, but it was the eighteenth century French philosopher Montesquieu who clearly defined three government functions and argued that separating those functions would best protect freedom and liberty. The Constitution's Framers agreed with Montesquieu.

How long did it take to develop the ideas found in the US Constitution?

The ideas found in the US Constitution evolved over a period of nearly two thousand years and lead to the creation of a representative republic.

Many of these ideas can be traced to the historian Polybius, who lived between 200–118 B.C. Polybius recognized the three principle forms of government that existed in his time: monarchy (rule by one), aristocracy (rule by few) and democracy (majority rule). He noted that all of these governments had problems.

Monarchs became tyrants. Aristocrats did little but secure their privileges. Monarchs and aristocrats would become the idle rich. In a democracy, majority rule turned into mob rule, trampling on the rights of minorities. The result of would be a "tyranny of the majority."

The Constitution's Framers read Polybius' writings. Trying to avoid the problems he described they created the American Republic nearly two thousand years later.

Who is most responsible for "separation of powers" in the American Constitution?

The French philosopher Montesquieu developed the separation of powers ideas, James Madison worked to put them into the Constitution.

Montesquieu built upon the work of the historian Polybius in writing his 1748 thesis *Spirit of the Laws*. Montesquieu identified government functions as legislative, executive and judicial. The Constitution's Framers, in writing the Constitution, relied greatly on Montesquieu.

In *Federalist No. 47*, James Madison cites Montesquieu as the author of separating the powers of government:

The oracle who is always consulted and cited on this subject is the celebrated Montesquieu. If he be not the author of this invaluable precept in the science of politics, he has the merit at least of displaying and recommending it most effectually to the attention of mankind.

Why do the members of Congress, the President and the Supreme Court serve different terms of office?

The Founders felt that officials with different interests would be less likely to join together and threaten the people's liberty.

James Madison, the Father of the American Constitution, came to the 1787 Convention hoping to build a government with the power to govern yet with limits on that power to protect liberty. Separating government functions would be one limit. Another limit would be that government officials performing these functions would be selected in different ways for different terms of service.

Madison explained the Constitution's design to protect liberty and the checks and balances built into the proposed constitution in *Federalist No. 51:*

... In order to lay a due foundation for that separate and distinct exercise of the different powers of government, which ... is ... essential to the preservation of liberty ... each department should have a will of its own ...

Is the idea of "separation of powers" the same as the idea of "checks and balances"?

No. Separation of powers divides the government based upon primary functions, legislative, executive and judicial, but these powers are not strictly separated. In some areas, overlapping powers are in place to "check" any one branch from having unrestrained power in a specific area and "balance" the government.

The president is part of the legislative process before a bill becomes law. The president may check Congress's power by a veto and a bill then only becomes law if two-thirds of the Senate and House vote to override the president. Congress can check the president's power by its control over the money available to the president. Congress can check the courts by defining their organization and the kinds of cases courts can decide. The president and the Senate jointly decide who will serve as judges. The courts may issues orders to the president and declare laws passed by Congress unconstitutional.

These "checks and balances" were designed as another layer of protection for the people's liberty.

Was separating power within the federal government enough protection for American liberty?

To protect liberty and freedom the Constitution's Framers established institutions to separate powers within the central government. For the revolutionary generation this was not enough.

In addition to separating powers inside the federal government limits on power from the outside were added as well. The states provided this limit by retaining every government power not granted to the federal government by the Constitution. Dividing power between different governments in the same territory was a unique creation: American Federalism.

The Tenth Amendment explains this best: *The powers not delegated to the United States by the Constitution, nor prohibited by it to the States, are reserved to the States respectively, or to the people.*

Separating power inside the federal government and dividing power between the federal government and the states provided two layers of protection for American liberty.

What is a constitution and what was the first written Constitution in the world?

A Constitution is a set of fundamental principles or established precedents according to which a state or other organization is governed.

The American Constitution was established through a ratification process involving the people. Seeking the consent of the people to be governed was consistent with the Declaration of Independence and unique to the United States.

The idea of the written constitution for a government started in America with the Fundamental Orders of Connecticut, which established the organization of that colony around 1638. The Fundamental Orders of Connecticut is considered to be the first *written* Constitution in world history. That is why Connecticut's nickname is the Constitution State.

Over the next 140 years, all the colonies came to rely upon written documents to organize their governments. These colonial experiences resulted in the 1787 Philadelphia Miracle: the United States Constitution.

Who wrote the final draft of the Constitution?

James Madison gave Gouverneur Morris credit for the final Constitution: *"The finish given to the style and arrangement of the Constitution fairly belongs to the pen of Mr. Morris."*

George Washington called the Constitutional Convention to order on May 25, 1787.

By September 8th, the Convention's work had resulted in a document of twenty-three unorganized articles with many amendments attempting to balance the needs of the states and the philosophy of the Declaration of Independence.

On September 8th a committee was formed to organize the Convention's work. The members were:

- Alexander Hamilton
- William Johnson
- Rufus King
- James Madison
- Gouverneur Morris

The committee turned the twenty-three articles into the Constitution's seven articles consisting of:

Article I, The Legislative Branch
Article II, The Executive Branch
Article III, The Judiciary
Article IV, The States
Article V, The Amendment Process
Article VI, The Legal Status of the Constitution
Article VII, Ratification

Thoughts on the Declaration of Independence

Why study the Declaration of Independence to understand the Constitution?

Study of the Declaration of Independence is crucial to understanding the Constitution. The Declaration told England's King George and the world why the colonies were separating from England. Importantly it also explained to the American people the philosophy of the new nation. Without an explanation to the people the new government would be without support.

For the first time in world history a country would be guided by a philosophy not based upon force, but upon a shared view of government's purpose. The Declaration defined government's purpose to secure our inalienable rights. The Constitution's purpose is to secure the blessings of liberty. To understand the Declaration of Independence is to understand the Constitution.

How are the Declaration of Independence and the Constitution connected?

The "self-evident" truths in the Declaration of Independence grow out of "the Law of Nature and of Nature's God . . ." The Natural Law referred to is recognized by the Constitution. This recognition was critical to balance the need for an organized society and every individual's natural desire for freedom.

The United States was founded on a philosophy. That philosophy contained the truths that human beings are equal in their possession of natural rights, such as the rights to life, liberty and property. The

Constitution is a set of rules to give life to the Declaration's central philosophy.

What is the "Law of Nature and Nature's God"?

There exist in the world things that no government has the power to change. No government can repeal the Law of Gravity. No government can extinguish the desire of human beings to be free. These are natural laws.

The Law of Nature is observable in a scientific sense. The Law of Nature's God is revealed to men in a spiritual sense. Whether scientific or spiritual, natural law comes to the same conclusion, that all men have inalienable rights. The Declaration of Independence relies upon this "self-evident" truth for the establishment of the United States.

Does the Constitution grant inalienable rights to Americans?

The Constitution does not grant inalienable rights. Such rights exist independent of the Constitution. An inalienable right belongs to every person simply by being born. These rights are not granted by government and cannot be given away.

The Constitution recognizes that inalienable rights exist and mentions some, for example: religion, speech and press. The Ninth Amendment points out that it is impossible to list every such right: "*The enumeration in the Constitution, of certain rights, shall not be construed to deny or disparage others retained by the people.*"

The Declaration of Independence recognizes every person's inalienable rights of "*Life, Liberty and the pursuit of Happiness*" and that the purpose of government is to secure those rights. The Constitution was "ordained and established" to create a government suited for that purpose.

How serious was the danger to the men signing the Declaration of Independence?

Consider the Declaration's final phrase: "*... with a firm reliance on the protection of divine Providence, we mutually pledge to each other our Lives, our Fortunes and our sacred Honor.*" The signers were committing treason against the King of England. The following was the penalty under English law:

1. That the offender be drawn to the gallows, and not be carried or walk; though usually a sledge or hurdle is allowed, to preserve the offender from the extreme torment of being dragged on the ground or pavement. 2. That he be hanged by the neck, and then cut down alive. 3. That his entrails be taken out, and burned, while he is yet alive. 4. That his head be cut off. 5. That his body be divided into four parts. 6. That his head and quarters be at the king's disposal.

The action to declare independence was not one taken lightly, and the commitment to the Declaration's principles of equality and the inalienable rights of men was clear.

What impact did the Declaration of Independence have upon the world?

"The American Declaration of 1776 was the first in world history to identify sovereignty with independence." —David Armitage

Before the Declaration of Independence, when people were dissatisfied with their "sovereign" or royal ruler, they made a deal with their current ruler or found a new one. A government typically was an empire controlled by a royal family. The American Declaration of Independence changed this, not just for America, but for the world.

In 1776 the Declaration of Independence was the first in history to declare a people free and self-governing. More declarations were soon to come. In 1790, the people of Flanders declared they were independent of the Austrian Emperor. The Haitian slave revolt was accompanied by a Declaration of Independence from France on January 1, 1804. There are now 195 countries in the world. More than 100 of them came into being with the issuance of a document whose heritage can be traced to the Declaration of Independence.

There was no precedent to begin a country based upon the *Laws of Nature and of Nature's God.* The successful revolution of the United States, announced by its Declaration of Independence, became a precedent for the world.

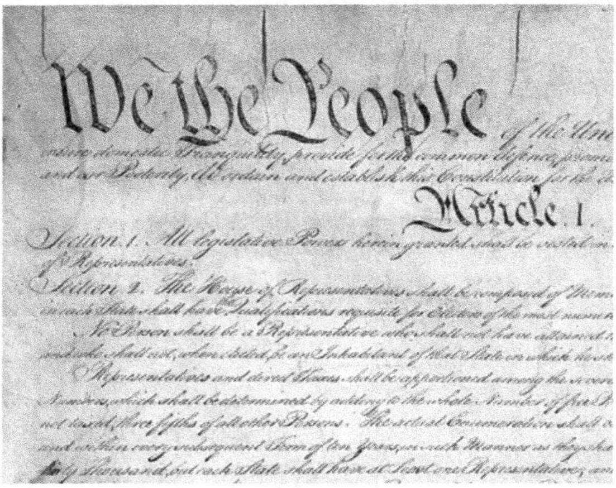
We the People
Article. 1.

The Constitution's Preamble

We the People of the United States, in Order to form a more perfect Union, establish Justice, insure domestic Tranquility, provide for the common defense, promote the general Welfare, and secure the Blessings of Liberty to ourselves and our Posterity, do ordain and establish this Constitution for the United States of America.

Who is responsible for the phrase "We the People of the United States"?

The Constitution's Preamble begins with the most famous phrase in United States history: "*We the people of the United States.*" The author of the phrase, Gouverneur Morris, was not among the Convention's most famous delegates.

On September 8, 1787 the constitution's elements had been agreed upon and a Committee on Style was tasked with turning those elements into a document. The initial draft started: "*We the people of the States of New Hampshire, Massachusetts . . .*"

Gouverneur Morris was assigned to draft and organize the Constitution. He changed the opening phrase to: "*We the People of the United States . . .*"

The change was important. Morris transformed the makers of the Constitution from the state governments to the PEOPLE of the UNITED STATES. This formed a single nation, the United States of America instead of an alliance of state governments.

By the way: Gouverneur was his first name, not his title.

Who created the United States?

The Constitution's Preamble has given Americans and people around the world the hope of a free and just society.

The Preamble states goals and also points out the obligations of the United States government to the American people. The Preamble defines the People as the creators of the United States. The United States as that creation owes loyalty to the People and a duty to follow their instructions.

What does the Preamble mean by a "more perfect union"?

Under the Articles of Confederation, the states had joined in *"a firm league of friendship, for their common defence, the security of their liberties, and their mutual and general welfare."* The agreement was among states, not people, and the union was weak and incomplete. The Preamble's statement refers to the Constitution's purpose of improving upon the Articles.

Modern readers likely think it impossible for something to be "more perfect." At the time of the Framing, perfect was not considered an absolute term. In the eighteenth century, "perfect" was still related to its Latin origin, *perficere*, to finish or complete. Thus "a more perfect union" was simply a more complete union than had existed before the Constitution.

What does the Preamble mean by "establish justice"?

In the second stated objective, to "establish Justice," the key word is "establish." The implication of the statement is that justice did not exist under the Articles of Confederation. The Framers had gathered from around the country and were aware of a problem. Although the individual American states and local governments had court systems with independent judges providing trial by jury, citizens traveling between states were not always treated fairly in the local courts.

Gouverneur Morris had chosen the word "justice" carefully. The lack of uniform "justice" throughout the country was clear to the Framers, and endangered individual liberties in many ways. To address this issue the Constitution created an independent Supreme Court with authority above the states and required the states to respect the privileges and immunities of United States citizens. These would be the means to "establish justice" for all citizens in the exercise of their inalienable rights.

What does the Preamble mean by "domestic tranquility"?

The Constitution was drafted only eleven years after Independence and four years after peace with England. English abuses of liberty were fresh for all the American people. They had not thrown off English chains to be now ruled by local tyrants. In 1786, Daniel Shays, a Revolutionary War Veteran had lead an armed rebellion against the tax policies and court procedures of Massachusetts. The Confederation Congress had no resources to restore "domestic tranquility," although ultimately a private Massachusetts militia did. This Massachusetts disturbance was a major impetus for the Constitutional Convention.

The armed revolt of war veterans against the state government shocked many. Keeping the peace and tranquility at home was an important concern. The Framers hoped a federal government with new powers and a uniform justice system protective of individual liberty would "insure domestic tranquility."

In a country born by revolt against oppressive government, such spirit remains alive, and the Constitution was drafted to balance that spirit with the benefits of civil society.

What type of threats existed for the new nation requiring "common defense"?

When the Constitution was being drafted, the new nation was in danger of attack from all sides. Spain claimed most of North America west of the Mississippi River, the Gulf Coast and Florida. Great Britain controlled Canada, and despite promises in the peace Treaty of Paris, maintained forts in areas between the Appalachians and the Mississippi River. Threats from hostile Native Americans existed on the frontier. No single state was capable of defending itself. The states needed each other to survive.

Despite the threats Americans maintained a fear of "standing armies," believing that armed forces sufficient to defend the nation would possess power to enslave it. Many Americans thought that, having won Independence over eighteenth century's super power Great Britain, guided by the Continental Congress, an American standing army was unnecessary and dangerous. The Framers, however, anticipated other wars and the need to be prepared to fight them. This anticipation overcame the fear of standing armies, but was balanced by a constitutional commitment to civilian control over any military needed for the "common defense."

What was "general welfare" as understood by the Framers?

"Promote the general welfare" had a well understood meaning at the time of the Constitution. "General" meant applicable to the whole rather than to individual, local or special interests. "Welfare" included the concept of "happiness" in addition to "well-being." A constitutional goal is to promote the happiness of the nation as a whole.

The Constitution's Tax and Spending Clause also contains the phrase "general welfare":

> *The Congress shall have Power To lay and collect Taxes, Duties, Imposts and Excises, to pay the Debts and provide for the common Defence and general Welfare of the United States."*
>
> — Article I, Section 8, Clause 1

While the Preamble gives no power to the federal government, it helps understand the rest of the Constitution. The Taxing and Spending Clause grants power with similar language.

In both instances "general" refers to the welfare of the United States as a whole, not the welfare of a personal, local or special interest. In supporting "general" welfare, the government is to create the environment that allows every individual to exercise his inalienable rights to life, liberty and the pursuit of happiness without interference.

What is the ultimate purpose of the Constitution as stated in the Preamble?

The constitutional goals to form a more complete union, establish a uniform system of justice throughout the country, provide people with safety and security both at home and from outside threats and promote the general happiness of the nation, are all elements to achieve a single purpose. That purpose is to *"secure the blessings of liberty,"* not only for the country's Founders, but for the generations to follow.

The Preamble introduces a document whose stated purpose is to secure the rights of life and liberty and promote national happiness. The Preamble as a whole, then, declares that the Constitution is designed to secure precisely the rights proclaimed in the Declaration of Independence. The Preamble proclaims the Constitution to be the fulfillment of the Declaration of Independence.

The Constitution's Preamble has stood as the mission statement of the United States since the Constitution was made public and sent to the states for ratification in September, 1787. Nearly every American student has spent time memorizing the paragraph. The opening three words: "We the People" have provided the inspiration for the growing inclusiveness in the American body politic for over two centuries.

Article I: The Congress

Why are the powers of Congress listed in the Constitution's Article I?

Article I Section 8 contains a list of specific congressional powers. The intent was to limit Congress to this list of "enumerated" powers.

Thirty-five constitutional convention delegates were lawyers. When a legal document lists powers, powers are limited to the list. The Constitution is a legal document. Listing congressional power was meant to limit government power in order to "secure the blessings of liberty."

When Congress acts outside the enumerated powers granted that act is unlawful or illegal. This is the essence of "limited government."

Article I is the Constitution's most detailed article. The Founders saw the legislature as the true source of government authority and in greatest need of limitations. The Congress is defined in Article I because as James Madison said, the Congress was "the first branch of government."

What are the powers of Congress listed in the Constitution?

The list of congressional powers is found in Article I, Section 8. These Enumerated Powers are to:

- Lay and collect taxes, duties, imposts and excises;
- Pay the debts and provide for the common defense and general welfare of the United States;
- Borrow money on the credit of the United States;
- Regulate commerce with foreign nations, and among the several states, and with the Indian tribes;

- Establish a uniform rule of naturalization, and uniform laws on the subject of bankruptcies throughout the United States;
- Coin money, regulate the value thereof, and of foreign coin, and fix the standard of weights and measures;
- Provide for the punishment of counterfeiting the securities and current coin of the United States;
- Establish post offices and post roads;
- Promote the progress of science and useful arts, by securing for limited times to authors and inventors the exclusive right to their respective writings and discoveries;
- Constitute tribunals inferior to the Supreme Court;
- Define and punish piracies and felonies committed on the high seas, and offenses against the law of nations;
- Declare war, grant letters of marque and reprisal, and make rules concerning captures on land and water;
- Raise and support armies, but no appropriation of money to that use shall be for a longer term than two years;
- Provide and maintain a navy;
- Make rules for the government and regulation of the land and naval forces;
- Provide for calling forth the militia to execute the laws of the union, suppress insurrections and repel invasions;
- Provide for organizing, arming, and disciplining, the militia;
- Exercise exclusive legislation in all cases whatsoever, over the seat of government;
- Make all laws which shall be necessary and proper for carrying into execution the foregoing powers.

What does it mean to say an act of Congress is "unconstitutional"?
When Congress passes a law outside the power granted in the Constitution it acts illegally and the law is unconstitutional. The Constitution's Article I Section 8 lists the subjects Congress may regulate by passing laws. The subjects include: interstate commerce, post offices, naturalization and more.

The last clause of Section 8 is known as the Necessary and Proper Clause. It reads:

To make all Laws which shall be necessary and proper for carrying into Execution the foregoing Powers

Section 8's final clause indicates that every law must be "necessary and proper" to the listed powers. An unnecessary or improper law is unconstitutional.

The Constitution exists to secure the blessings of liberty for the people and their posterity. Such liberty is secure only when government operates within constitutional limits.

Did the Constitution ever limit federal office holders by gender, race or ethnic background?

The Constitution never contained gender, ethnic or property requirements for national office.

The Constitution's Article I Defines the House of Representatives. The House of Representatives is made up of members from each state according to a state's population determined every ten years in the census. These qualifications are required to serve in the House:

- Twenty-five years of age
- Seven years a citizen of the United States
- An inhabitant of the state from which elected

The qualifications are straightforward, and forward-looking. In 1787, when the Constitution was written, voting by women and non-whites was nearly non-existent. In most states only property owners could hold office.

The Constitution's Framers, sometimes discredited as a bunch of rich old white guys, looked forward to a time when women and citizens of every race would be full participants in the national government.

How many members does the House of Representatives have?

Article I, Section 2, defines the way in which congressional districts are to be divided among the states. This section establishes that every ten years a census of the people of the United States must be conducted.

From the census Congress determines how many members of the House of Representatives are to come from each state. The census is also used to determine how federal resources are to be distributed among the states.

The Constitution set the number of House members from each of the original thirteen states that was used until the first census was completed. There were sixty-five members of the First Congress. As the US population grew the number of House members grew until 1929. That year Congress limited the House of Representatives to 435 members and established a formula to determine how many districts would be in each state. The number remains 435 today. After each census the number of representatives may go up or down depending on shifts in population.

Did the Constitution place specific limits on Congress?
The unamended Constitution specifically prohibits Congress from doing the following:

- Suspending the writ of *habeas corpus*
- Taxing the ports of one state more than the ports of another
- Passing bills of attainder or *ex post facto* laws
- Spending funds without passing a law allowing it to do so
- Granting titles of nobility

Habeas Corpus requires the government to explain to a judge why it is restricting someone's freedom, or else set that person free. Prohibitions on Bills of Attainder and *ex post facto* laws prevent Congress from singling out a particular person for punishment, or making conduct illegal after it takes place.

The prohibition on titles of nobility recognizes the American belief, stated in the Declaration of Independence that "all men are created equal."

Further limits would be added by the Bill of Rights, which begins: "*Congress shall make no law . . .*"

Are there divisions of power within the Congress?

There are principles embodied in the US Constitution, derived from the Declaration of Independence. These principles contributed to the establishment of separation of powers, checks and balances and federalism, all to protect liberty. The Framers were so concerned about the dangers of power, they even divided certain functions between the House and the Senate.

Government's greatest power and threat to liberty and natural rights is the power to tax. The Framers wanted taxation subject to the closest possible scrutiny by the voters. Citizens would elect Members of the House of Representatives every two years from local districts.

The Constitution's Article I, Section 7, Clause 1, known as the "Origination Clause" provides:

All bills for raising revenue shall originate in the House of Representatives; but the Senate may propose or concur with amendments as on other Bills.

The Origination Clause gave the "power of the purse" to the part of government designed to be closest to the people. The plan was to provide clear accountability and a short time frame for citizens to be heard on taxes by way of their ballots, and another division of power within the legislative branch.

Can Congress pass a law just because it is favored by a majority of the people?

For Congress to legally pass a law, it must have authority granted by the Constitution. If the power has not been granted, it does not matter if a majority are in favor of the law.

Often there are calls for Congress to "do something" about a problem. Such calls for Congress to act fail to consider that "we the people" may not have given it the power over the "problem."

Article I's list of powers are the primary source of constitutional authority granted by the people.

The term "granted" is critical. Congress only has the power that "we the people" have given it in the Constitution. If it's not on the list, Congress cannot legally do "it," even if a majority of the people want "it" done. This is to prevent a "tyranny of the majority" that would trample on minority rights, an intricate protection for the inalienable rights of the Declaration of Independence.

Are congressional powers and restrictions the only subjects of the Constitution's Article I?

No, Article I also places important limits on state governments. Before the Constitution each state was its own little country rather than part of a larger nation. A "more perfect union" required states to stop being separate countries. Article I, Section 10 prohibited states from actions that had international impact:

- entering into any Treaty, Alliance, or Confederation;
- granting Letters of Marque and Reprisal;
- coining Money or emitting Bills of Credit;
- make any Thing but gold and silver Coin a Tender in Payment of Debts;
- passing any Bill of Attainder, ex post facto Law, or Law impairing the Obligation of Contracts,
- granting any Title of Nobility.
- laying any Imposts or Duties on Imports or Exports,

And states would need the Consent of Congress to

- lay any Duty of Tonnage,
- keep Troops, or Ships of War in time of Peace,
- enter into any Agreement or Compact with another State, or with a foreign Power,
- engage in War, unless actually invaded, or in such imminent Danger as will not admit of delay.

With these limits on states, the United States could now speak to the world with a single voice and become the Preamble's more perfect union.

Article II: The President

Why does the office of the president have such great power?
The unspoken expectation of the Constitution's writers in creating this powerful office was that a person they could trust, George Washington, would be the first president. The people who had fought a war to rid themselves of a king created a president with great authority. The power of the president is a result of the faith placed in Washington.

The United States President is called the most powerful individual in the world. The source of this power is the Constitution's Article II.

Article II uses about 1000 words to define the term of office, the selection, qualifications, oath, responsibilities and impeachment provisions. It starts simply:

The executive power shall be vested in a President of the United States of America.

Do the American people directly vote for their president?

The short answer is "no."

The Constitution's Article II created the Electoral College for electing the president. Each state has electors equal to its number of Senators and Representatives. The Constitution lets states determine how Electors are chosen. Once chosen, a college member may constitutionally vote for anyone for president.

Electors are now chosen by popular vote by state with citizens actually voting for electors pledged to a presidential candidate. This system may result in a presidential candidate winning the people's vote yet losing in the Electoral College. This happened in 1876, 1888 and 2000 and is the source of efforts to reform the presidential election process. Opponents of reform believe that if presidents were elected by a simple popular majority, a candidate could win with concentration on only major population centers and ignore other parts of the country with varying interests.

What are the qualifications to be president?

There were only three original Constitutional qualifications to be president. An individual must be:

- A natural born citizen of the United States
- Thirty-five years of age
- Fourteen years a resident of the United States

The Twenty-Second Amendment, in setting presidential term limits, added another qualification. Anyone who has previously served more than six years as president may not be elected to that office again.

The presidential oath is the only oath of office specifically defined by the Constitution. No one may become president without taking this oath:

I do solemnly swear that I will faithfully execute the office of President of the United States, and will to the best of my ability, preserve, protect and defend the Constitution of the United States.

Did the original Constitution provide that the vice-president became president if the president died?

The Constitution did not say that if a president died the vice-president would become president, only that the powers of the president would "devolve upon the Vice-President."

On April 4, 1841 William Henry Harrison became the first president to die in office. The Constitution did not address questions regarding the status of Vice-President John Tyler. When Harrison died Tyler's constitutional status was unclear. Was Tyler president or Vice-President acting as president? Was there a difference?

Tyler acted to resolve one constitutional question, apparently for personal, not constitutional reasons. Tyler decided he was president and took the presidential oath. The difference: a president was paid $25,000 and the vice-president was paid only $5,000. Tyler's pay increased by five times. All vice-presidents followed the precedent until the Twenty-Fifth Amendment finally addressed the subject.

What limits the president's powers granted by the Constitution?

Though the Constitution grants great presidential power, such power remains limited. He can do no more than the Constitution allows and only the Congress can provide the money for the president to exercise any of his powers.

The Constitution's Article II, defines the president's authority and appoints him the military's Commander in Chief. As commander of the world's most powerful military he is known as the world's most powerful leader.

The President's control over the executive branch comes from his power, with the consent of the Senate, to appoint: "officers of the United States." These officers generally serve at the President's pleasure (except judges, who have lifetime appointments).

The President represents the United States to other nations due to the constitutional power to negotiate treaties, with Senate approval.

The President's pardon power allows him to call off an execution or free someone from prison.

How were leaders of countries removed from office before the Constitution's provision for presidential impeachment?

Benjamin Franklin noted that in world history there had been but one way to remove a government leader: assassinate him. (Think Julius Caesar.) Franklin pointed out to the Constitutional Convention that presidents might *"render [themselves] obnoxious."* The convention saw Franklin's point and included the impeachment provisions.

Article II contains the Constitution's Impeachment Clause:

The President, Vice President and all civil officers of the United States, shall be removed from office on impeachment for, and conviction of, treason, bribery, or other high crimes and misdemeanors.

Defining a high crime or misdemeanor has proved difficult. Practically, those offenses amount to conduct agreed upon by a majority of the House and two-thirds of the Senate.

The idea that a country's leader could be removed without being killed was novel to the world.

What Can a President Legally Do With a Pen and a Phone?

In January, 2014 President Obama brought national attention to the idea of a president running the country by "executive order" with his now famous statement: "I've got a pen and I've got a phone." During his 2014 State of the Union speech President Obama asserted his authority in even stronger terms: "wherever and whenever I can take steps without legislation . . . that's what I'm going to do."

Though the United States does not have a king, but rather a president, the Constitution grants many presidential powers and Congress by law has delegated others. Presidential directives, orders or proclamations directly affecting the lives of individual Americans must be judged by a president's legal authority to issue them.

When the President issues an executive order, the legal authority for that order must come from provisions in the Constitution or authority given to the President by law from Congress. An order issued outside those categories is likely illegal and unconstitutional.

The following presidential functions mentioned in the Constitution provide authority for the President to issue some directives:

He can issue directives as:

- Commander in Chief of the Armed Forces
- Head of the Executive Branch (State, Defense, Treasury, etc.)
- Chief Law Enforcement Officer of the United States
- Head of State (principally in charge of foreign affairs)

In the *lawful* exercise of one of these functions, presidential power to issue orders is broad. The President also may issue directives in the exercise of authority delegated through law by Congress. Congress may limit delegations in law to be exercised only in a particular way.

Is there a test to determine if a president has acted illegally?
In 1952, President Harry Truman ordered a government takeover of the country's steel mills. The Supreme Court determined Truman's order was illegal. Supreme Court Justice Robert Jackson explained how to determine if a presidential order is illegal:

Justice Jackson's Standards for Use of Presidential Power

1. **When the President acts pursuant to an express or implied authorization of Congress, his authority is at its maximum.** A presidential order authorized by Congress will be constitutional, unless Congress itself had acted unconstitutionally.
2. **When the President acts in absence of either a congressional grant or denial of authority, he can only rely upon his own independent powers.** Such independent power comes from his constitutional duties. These powers are limited by the constitutional separation of power between the executive, the Congress and the courts.

3. When the President takes measures incompatible with the expressed or implied will of Congress, his power is at its lowest ebb. Under this scenario, it is likely the president has acted in an unconstitutional manner and his order is illegal.

Article III: The Supreme Court

Are members of the Supreme Court required to be lawyers?

Article III, created the Supreme Court but set no qualifications for United States judges. Judges are not required to be lawyers.

While Articles I and II define the election of the president and members of Congress, Article III does not mention the selection of judges, nor even the office of Chief Justice. The president's power to appoint judges with the advice and consent of the Senate is found in Article II, Section 2 under presidential powers. The Constitution does not address the organization of the courts, provide for the number of Supreme Court justices and does not establish trial or appellate courts. These matters are left to the Congress. Article III, in establishing the third branch of government is interesting for what it does not say, as well as for what it says.

Did the Constitution define the organization of the federal courts?
The Constitution provides almost no detail on the federal courts, and leaves most of that work to Congress.

The Constitution's Article III creates the Supreme Court, provides for lifetime appointment of federal judges and prohibits Congress from decreasing judicial pay.

> "*The judicial Power of the United States, shall be vested in one supreme Court, and in such inferior Courts as the Congress may from time to time ordain and establish. The Judges, both of the supreme and inferior Courts, shall hold their Offices during good Behavior, and shall, at stated Times, receive for their Services a Compensation which shall not be diminished during their Continuance in Office.*"

The Constitution allows Congress to set the Supreme Court's size, schedule, and organization. The Constitution assumes there will be a Chief Justice, but did not create the office, only mentioning it as the official presiding at presidential impeachments.

The Framers thought the judicial branch was least likely to endanger the people's freedom, and gave it the least attention.

How are the federal courts organized?
The Constitution's Article III created the Supreme Court and authorized Congress to establish a system of lower courts. Currently there are ninety-four district level trial courts and thirteen courts of appeals below the Supreme Court.

The thirteen appellate courts below the US Supreme Court are called the US Circuit Courts of Appeals. The ninety-four federal judicial districts are organized into twelve regional circuits, each of which has a court of appeals. Appellate courts decide whether or not a trial court correctly applied the law. Appeals courts consist of three judges and do not use a jury.

A court of appeals hears challenges to district court decisions and appeals from decisions of federal administrative agencies.

The nation's ninety-four district or trial courts are called US District Courts. District courts resolve disputes by determining the facts and applying legal principles to decide who is right. In most cases in the trial courts, the people involved have the right to a trial by jury.

How are Supreme Court and other federal judges chosen?

While the Constitution provides detailed qualifications for the House of Representatives, the Senate, and the presidency, it does not set any standards for federal judges. Once someone becomes a federal judge, the only requirement to keep the job is to exhibit "good behavior."

The Constitution gives the responsibility for nominating federal judges and Supreme Court Justices to the president. The president's nominations must be confirmed by the Senate.

A president has available many resources to rely upon for selecting judicial nominees. The Department of Justice, the Federal Bureau of Investigation, members of Congress, sitting judges and justices, and the American Bar Association provide the president with suggestions and research.

The Senate's constitutional role in approving judges gave rise to an important tradition in the appointment of federal district court judges. The practice is referred to as senatorial courtesy. When a judicial vacancy occurs in a state whose senators belong to the same political party as the president, the senators send a recommendation to the president. The president nearly always follows the recommendation.

What kinds of cases can the federal courts decide?

Article III, Section 2 defines the types of cases that federal courts may decide. The federal courts can only hear those cases involving subjects defined in the Constitution and refined by Congress. This concept is known as subject matter jurisdiction. This is in contrast to state courts that can hear nearly every type of controversy. State courts are courts of general jurisdiction. Federal courts are considered to be courts of "limited jurisdiction." Federal courts can make decisions in the following types of cases:

- cases arising under the Constitution, laws, and treaties of the United States (Federal question jurisdiction)
- cases involving ambassadors, other public ministers and consuls (Ambassador jurisdiction)
- cases involving navigable waters (Admiralty jurisdiction)
- cases in which the United States is a party (United States as a party jurisdiction)
- cases between two or more states (State jurisdiction)
- cases between citizens of different states (Diversity jurisdiction)
- cases between citizens of the same state claiming land under the grants of different states (Land grants jurisdiction)
- cases between a state or citizens of a state and a foreign state or citizens of a foreign state (Alienage jurisdiction)

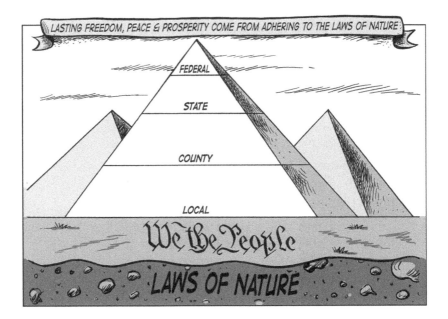

LASTING FREEDOM, PEACE & PROSPERITY COME FROM ADHERING TO THE LAWS OF NATURE

FEDERAL

STATE

COUNTY

LOCAL

We the People

LAWS OF NATURE

Article IV: Government Relations

Why can a driver's license issued by one state be used in another?
Because the Constitution requires each state to recognize the official
acts of all the other states.

Article IV begins with this sentence: "*Full Faith and Credit shall be
given in each State to the public Acts, Records, and judicial Proceedings
of every other State.*"

When a citizen resolves an issue within one of the States that resolution must be recognized by all other States. The Full Faith and Credit
Clause guarantees this. Without that clause a state might not recognize a marriage, divorce, driver's license, birth record or other actions
resolved in another state.

The US Constitution's Article IV defines relationships among the
governments regarding the following: recognition of each government's
official acts, how a State treats the citizens of another state, extradi-
tion of criminal fugitives, return of slaves, admission of new States,
and defense of the country from invasion and domestic violence. This
Article provides legal definitions for parts of American federalism.

Must a state treat citizens of other states the same as it treats its own citizens?
The Constitution's "Privileges and Immunities" Clause requires a State to treat citizens of other States as it treats its own citizens.

The Constitution's Article IV, Section 2 provides: *"The Citizens of each State shall be entitled to all Privileges and Immunities of Citizens in the several States."* These "privileges and immunities" include:

- protection by the Government
- the enjoyment of life and liberty
- the right of a citizen of one State to pass through
- the benefits of the writ of *habeas corpus*
- pursuing lawsuits of any kind in the courts of the State
- owning and disposing of property, either real or personal

These constitutional requirements are benefits conferred on twenty-first century Americans by the eighteenth century drafters of the Constitution.

What is the power of Congress to admit new states to the union?
Article IV Section 3 gave Congress the power to admit new states, providing the basis for the growth to today's fifty states. While Section 3 gives Congress wide latitude in admitting new states to the Union, Article IV, Section 4 commands: *"The United States shall guarantee to every State in this Union a Republican Form of Government."*

For a State to be admitted to the Union, it must establish a representative or republican government. This means a government that is made up of representatives, rather than the alternative of "direct democracy." Direct democracy is when all eligible citizens vote on every law.

The only other limitations were that there could be no new State formed within the borders of an existing State or by combining two States without legislative approval of the States involved. This provision came into play when West Virginia was formed from part of Virginia during the Civil War.

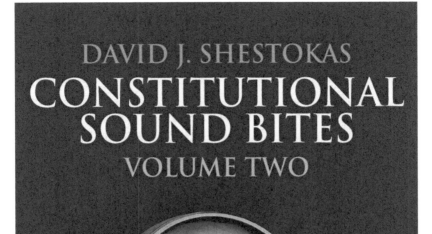

DAVID J. SHESTOKAS

CONSTITUTIONAL
SOUND BITES

VOLUME TWO

TO MY DAD, TOM SHESTOKAS, HIS FELLOW WORLD
WAR II VETERANS AND ALL WHO HAVE RISKED THEIR
LIVES, FORTUNES AND SACRED HONOR FOR THE IDEALS
THAT CREATED THE UNITED STATES OF AMERICA

CONSTITUTIONAL SOUND BITES

VOLUME TWO

DAVID J. SHESTOKAS

CONSTITUTIONALLY SPEAKING
Lemont, IL

Introduction, Volume Two

This series, *Constitutional Sound Bites*, is an effort to reveal the grand concepts in the documents that bind America, the Declaration of Independence and the Constitution, in a way that fits with how we have come to communicate in the twenty-first century. We seldom have long detailed philosophical discussion about liberty and justice and the goals of our government. Most information available these days comes in short tweets or a few minutes on the news or YouTube. This series attempts to take important ideas from America's Founding and condense them to a format more like how we communicate today.

There is danger and difficulty in the effort. The danger is that the subjects deserve more detail than the format allows. The difficulty is that the short modern format of sound bites, tweets and headlines is more suited to entertain than inform. The challenge is to present sufficient detail in a short form that can both entertain and inform.

The subject matter is important enough to make the effort to combine brevity, clarity and accuracy in a way to interest the reader to learn more. For the reader interested in learning more, there are some links to additional information. This also is consistent with the modern world.

America was gifted with a government devoted to freedom. We cannot allow it to drift away in the mist of time or become like a mythology that was not real because the eighteenth century presentation is foreign to the modern ear.

America's founding documents, the Declaration of Independence and the Constitution, contain grand concepts. Some of those concepts are stated obviously: "*all men are created equal.*" Many are hidden in phrases like: "*All legislative Powers herein granted shall be vested in a Congress of the United States . . .*" The ideals so clearly stated in the

Declaration of Independence and the Constitution's Preamble can be found in the DNA of phrases that begin like *"All legislative powers..."* *Constitutional Sound Bites* reveals some of that DNA.

Getting Through the Legal Documents to the Purpose

When was the last time you read a criminal complaint just for fun or sat down with a power of attorney just for entertainment or education? The answer is likely never. The reality is that the Declaration of Independence is modeled after a criminal complaint, and the Constitution is modeled after a Power of Attorney. Reading a legal document for grins or enlightenment does not consume most folks on a Saturday night or any other night.

Reading such documents for information happens sometimes, but even then, it's more likely that there's a request for professional help to understand what the document means, because, like every occupation in life, the law has its own language. The words are there for a purpose and sometimes mean things that are clear to a lawyer and not clear to the rest of the world.

This is not peculiar to the law. Auto mechanics have their own language as do cooks, nurses, doctors, firemen, computer programmers and police. There are abbreviations that mean things to us in our work that mean little to anyone else. These shortcuts can be full of meaning to the people using them, but utterly meaningless to the rest of us.

These special phrases, "terms of art," abbreviations and "jargon" are usually filled with meaning to the people in a line of work. They aid people in getting a job done by communicating complex thoughts in short expressions, quickly and easily to others in their field. The ideas behind the words are well understood by the people that need the understanding.

After all, few of us will ever need to align the wheels of a car, prepare a soufflé, give a vaccination, find someone in a burning building, debug a website or determine if there's reason to arrest someone. There are people with special training to do those things to help society run.

This is also the case in the law and works well when judges and lawyers are speaking to each other. However, every American has a vote, and to properly exercise their vote they should not need to consult an attorney on the meaning of their Declaration of Independence or Constitution.

The Declaration of Independence and the Constitution are legal documents. Lawyers had a great deal of input in creating them. Twenty-four of the Declaration's fifty-eight signers were lawyers. Thirty-five of the delegates to the 1787 Constitutional Convention were lawyers. Both documents use legal terms that had special meaning in the eighteenth century, and continue to have such meanings today.

Legal Rules for Reading the Documents as Understood by the Framers

Besides the legal terms used in the documents, there are "legal rules for reading" documents. One of the most important rules for reading the Constitution was used by the drafters and relied upon by the Constitution's supporters during the ratification debates. The Federalists actually relied upon the Latin phrase for the rule: *"Expressio unius est exclusio alterius."* In English this means: *"the express mention of one thing excludes all others."*

Based on that legal rule for reading documents, the Constitution's supporters argued that because the document listed specific powers, the proposed government could not exercise any other powers. To objections that the Constitution did not contain a Bill of Rights providing protections for important rights such as religion, press or speech the Constitution's supporters replied there was no need for such protections. They referred to the rule and said because the document listed the subjects of government power and the list did not provide power over religion, speech or press the government could not intrude upon these freedoms.

Reliance on a legal rule was not enough for the Constitution's opponents. They wanted much stronger protections for natural rights than a Latin phrase. Their objections would result in the Bill of Rights.

This Latin phrase is but one example of the concepts built into the founding documents that are not obviously mentioned in them. There are others such as fiduciary, principal, agent and more. These are among the hidden ideas that join the grand concepts stated in the Declaration of Independence and the Preamble.

The series *Constitutional Sound Bites*, among its other goals, tries to translate some of these ideas into common language.

Constitutional Sound Bites, the Series

The first volume of this series, *Constitutional Sound Bites, Volume One* emphasizes the philosophy of the Declaration of Independence and the Constitution with only a few entries devoted to the procedures or technical aspects of the government created by the Constitution.

Constitutional Sound Bites, Volume Two maintains the emphasis of *Volume One* on the reasons WHY words and phrases are in the Declaration of Independence and Constitution. There are also more entries that address technical matters like the length of terms for members of the House and Senate. Even as the technical matters like the power of Congress to pass laws or the president's command of the armed forces come up, the relationship of those technicalities to the recurring themes of liberty and our inalienable rights remain the focus.

James Madison said: *"Every word of the Constitution decides a question between power and liberty."* The question was always how to give the government enough power to be an effective protector of liberty and yet restrict that power from becoming a threat to liberty. The entries in *Constitutional Sound Bites* are an effort to explain how the design of government was meant to minimize government's threat to freedom.

This series is to provide Americans with something our educational system seems to have allowed to fall by the wayside. There are some who believe that leaving out civics classes has been by design over the last several generations with the purpose of "fundamentally transforming America." It's unlikely that evil conspiracies exist that purposely result in the lack of education on these matters as part of some malicious plot to undermine America.

It is more likely that in the modern day the origins of America have been taken for granted. It is now truly centuries that have passed between the struggles of the founding and the incredible ideas that arose from that era and the twenty-first century. The generations of Americans that followed the Founding began seeking to leave their own stamp on the American story. In doing so, there was less concentration on distant history and an assumption that the gifts we were given would continue to have the desired effect of freedom.

Americans need to be forever mindful that incredible historical forces came together that resulted in what was then a revolutionary idea: *"All men are created equal."* When one thinks of the eighteenth century world of castes, nobility and servants, owners and slaves, landlords and serfs and indentured servants, it is clear that the concept of equality was heresy to many, both in America and around the world.

In the 238+ years since the Declaration of Independence, the concept that all are created equal has now evolved to be neither heresy nor revolutionary but considered common sense in much of the world. While this is now the conventional wisdom, the efforts to make it reality must continue. There remain men with a desire to exercise power over others. Such men will always be with us. That being the case, it is always necessary to study the times and documents that gave birth to the concept and the institutions that were created to make the concept real. There is truth to the idea that: *"Those who do not remember the past are condemned to repeat it."*

A Touch of History, a Bit of Philosophy and Institutions

With that in mind, grasping the founding documents requires three levels of understanding. The history of the times, the underlying philosophy and the mechanical institutions created to give effect to the philosophy in the world.

One needs to know the *"School House Rock"* details of how a bill becomes a law. That is not enough. Equally as critical is to know why those rules exist. What are they designed to achieve? The short answer is: A country ruled by law, not by men, and laws that are derived from the consent of the governed. Only in such a world can all men be equal. Not in terms of skills, knowledge or other attributes, but in terms of being treated equally by the law.

The Loss of the Common Heritage of Americans

As new generations arrive they want to leave their own mark on America, and think that new ideas are necessarily better than old ones. Our history becomes a mythology of dates, places and battles rather than of ideas. The result has been a lack of education on the ideas that drove America to its special place in the world. We are worse off for that in several ways.

One is that it was the commonality of founding ideas that actually made a nation out of a diverse set of people. It may be difficult to comprehend today, but when most eighteenth century Americans talked of their country, the reference was to their home states like Virginia or New York. It was the founding ideas that made a country.

If we lose touch with those ideas, we lose the thing that has bound the country over its existence. If we are to remain a nation we must refresh the ideas not only in ourselves but in each other. Taking time to pick up an idea, even a minute here or there in our busy lives, and sharing it with others creates new bonds.

James Madison writes in Federalist 51 that *"Men are not angels; their passions and self-interest often get the better of their reason and sense of justice, so we need government in order to protect our rights against those who would take them away."* Having noted that men are not angels Madison also writes, *"Government must be limited because people in government have passions and interests too."*

Madison's understanding of human nature is built into the Constitution as "separation of powers," "checks and balances," and "federalism." Many Americans today forget this, thinking we can do away with constitutional limits on government. We fail to study the purpose of those phrases at our peril.

Supreme Court Opinions are Not the Constitution
You will find only a rare Supreme Court opinion mentioned in this series. Supreme Court opinions are constitutional law, but they are not the Constitution. The Constitution is the effort to put into practice the principles of its Preamble and the Declaration of Independence. It is knowledge of those ideals and principles that allows a free people to govern themselves and to fairly judge if the Supreme Court is doing a good job.

Constitutional Considerations, Volume Two

Reading the Constitution gets off to a wonderful start with the Preamble's soaring statement of purpose. After that much of it reads like a technical legal document, which it is. It becomes more entertaining when you look for the goals to be achieved with separation of powers, American Federalism or republican principles. It becomes like a jigsaw puzzle with tiny pieces that fit together to meet the goals of the Preamble. This section, Constitutional Considerations, points out some of the puzzle pieces to help see how other aspects of the Constitution fit together to reveal a limited government that provides maximum freedom.

What is a Republic?

The United States is a republic. In a republic the people choose representatives to exercise their power. A republic does not have a king or queen, but rather an elected or appointed president. A republic starts with a free individual with the right to govern himself. That individual gives some of that power to the community. The community chooses representatives to serve in government and gives those representatives the power to make laws. That power is to make laws only about those subjects that the community has identified.

The elements of a republic are these: 1) a representative government, 2) a written constitution and 3) the rule of law. The rule of law requires that no one be above the law and that the rights of minorities are protected.

The source of authority in a republic is the people as a whole, and the people as a whole ratify, or agree to, a constitution before it becomes effective. A republic does not operate under the 50% + 1 rule by design in order to limit the government's power and to protect "natural rights."

What is Democracy?

In a democracy citizens exercise power directly. In a pure democracy, 50% of the group plus one more citizen determine the laws. There are no protections for minority rights. Minorities have only those privileges granted by the good graces of the majority.

In its pure form, democracy is simply majority rule. All citizens get together to decide every issue of government. Decisions made by 50% + 1 of those participating are binding on everyone. Pure democracy is sometimes referred to as "mobocracy" because decisions are made by a simple majority of a mob and enforced on everyone.

Did the Constitution establish a democracy for the United States?

The Constitution created a republic.

Ben Franklin famously replied when asked about the government that was created by the Constitution: "*A republic, if you can keep it.*" The US is a Constitutional Republic, not a "democracy." Here's Franklin's description of democracy: *"Democracy is two wolves and a lamb voting on what to have for dinner."*

No American founding document, not the Declaration of Independence, the Articles of Confederation, or the Constitution mention "democracy." In contrast, the Constitution's Article IV requires every state to be a republic.

Thomas Jefferson thought democracies were dangerous because: *"A democracy is nothing more than mob rule, where fifty-one percent of the people may take away the rights of the other forty-nine."*

John Adams knew democracies had short lives: *"Remember, democracy never lasts long. It soon wastes, exhausts, and murders itself. There never was a democracy yet that did not commit suicide."*

What does the Preamble mean by "the general welfare"?
The Constitution's Framers understood general welfare to be the public good or happiness. The Constitution's Preamble speaks about promoting the general welfare. This comes from the Declaration of Independence statement that government's purpose is to secure for each citizen his natural rights to life, liberty, and the pursuit of happiness.

To achieve that purpose the powers of the federal government were listed, enumerated and limited. All other issues were reserved to those governments closest to the people: the states. This was designed to secure rights recognized in the Declaration. The public good or "general welfare" was to be promoted by securing the inalienable rights of all Americans.

Why are there three branches of government?
The short answer is to protect liberty. To provide this protection power was divided within the federal government. The Founders knew that if the government was controlled by one man or one group that the United States would wind up under the rule of another dictator or tyrant.

To avoid the risk of a dictator, the new government was divided into three parts, or branches: the legislative, executive and the judicial. Different people would make the law (legislative), enforce the law (executive) and interpret the law (judicial). No single person or persons would have all the power of government.

All three branches are similarly responsible to the people. Each branch can do no more than constitutionally allowed and in those limitations are the protections for our liberty.

What is important about American Federalism?

American Federalism was a unique development that can be traced to the General Orders of Connecticut in 1639. The Constitution's Framers viewed federalism as a crucial value for the protection of liberty in a vast republic. Dividing power between the Federal, state, and local governments, was a liberty protection in addition to dividing power within the federal government between the three branches.

National matters involving relations with foreign countries and defense are best suited to national solutions addressed by the Federal Government. State and local governments, being closest to the people, are far more appropriate to manage local questions. This extra division of power between governments was designed to add protection for the natural rights of the people.

Thoughts on the Declaration of Independence, Volume Two

The Declaration of Independence not only announced that the colonies were leaving the British Empire. It also stated the new nation's guiding principles. It was unprecedented to found a country based upon a philosophy that started with "all men are created equal." This "self-evident" truth and others expressed in the Declaration are at work in the Constitution.

In what way are all men created equal?

The Declaration of Independence asserts all men are created equal. Every human is equal in having the same natural and inalienable rights. All people are to be treated equally by the law without regard to religion, sex, or ethnicity.

America's Founders knew that people do not have equal physical and mental talents. Such differences have no bearing on their natural rights. Differences among people do not give one person a right to rule over anyone else. All men and women are born with the same natural rights as any other person, simply by being human.

Abraham Lincoln said that the principle of equal rights, "clears the path for all—gives hope to all, and, by consequence, enterprise, and industry to all." To have equal rights is to have equal opportunity in the pursuit of happiness and to be treated equally by the law. That is how we are all created equal.

What are inalienable, natural rights?

The Declaration of Independence proclaims that all people are born with inalienable natural rights. These include the rights to life, liberty and property. (Jefferson changed John Locke's "property" to the "*pursuit of happiness*") These rights are natural to the condition of being human.

One who lives by this principle demands nothing of others except a mutual respect of those rights. Natural rights are not claims upon the property or resources of others. Protection of such rights requires only cooperation.

No government grants natural rights and no government can legitimately take them away. No person can give them away. This is the meaning of "inalienable."

Why does government exist?

The Declaration of Independence declares: "*Governments are instituted among Men*" to secure their natural rights. Over history, governments were started to safeguard people from clashes, to provide security and for the powerful to exercise control over the weak.

The Declaration of Independence has a different purpose for government: the protection of natural rights from others who would attempt to take such rights away.

Throughout history people have struggled for power. People started societies for protection, but the powerful ruled in those societies, often ignoring the rights of those being ruled, and called it "government." The Declaration of Independence explains this and concludes that the only legitimate government derives its "*just powers from the consent of the governed*."

What is the Consent of the Governed?

The Declaration of Independence, with the phrase *"consent of the governed,"* expresses the belief that a government's legal and ethical authority is limited. Government's use of power over the lives of people is only lawful when the people have consented to allowing government to deprive someone of life, liberty or property.

The people consented to the Constitution by the process of ratification. The Constitution provided for periodic elections and amendments. With elections and amendments the Constitution affords renewal of the consent that first took place with ratification.

These provisions for renewal of consent are protections for liberty, but Thomas Jefferson was aware that even elections were not a guarantee that government power would not be abused. In writing about the dangers of an elected aristocracy Jefferson said: *"173 despots would surely be as oppressive as one."*

The procedures alone do not assure ongoing consent. It must be earned by government each and every day.

What are "self-evident" truths?

An idea is self-evident if it can be taken for granted and is in no need of proof or explanation. The Declaration of Independence is built around concepts that are undoubtedly true at first impression to any reasonable person.

The United States Declaration of Independence, states: *"We hold these Truths to be self-evident, that all men are created equal, that they are endowed by their Creator with certain unalienable Rights that among these are Life, Liberty and the Pursuit of Happiness."*

These truths may be accepted as self-evident in much of the world now. In 1776 when monarchies were the norm and slavery was legal, the accepted truth was that some were born better than others. The Declaration of Independence began to change that and the change is ongoing.

What is the Right of Revolution?

Among the rights included in the Declaration of Independence is one frequently overlooked: The Right of Revolution. After discussing the purpose of government, the Declaration states: *"whenever any Form of Government becomes destructive of these ends, it is the Right of the People to alter or to abolish it, and to institute new Government . . ."*

Thomas Jefferson stated quite clearly the right of the people of a nation to overthrow a government that acts against their common interests.

John Locke, from whom Jefferson borrowed extensively put it this way in his Second *Treatise of Civil Government*: *"whenever the Legislators endeavor to take away, and destroy the Property of the People, or to reduce them to Slavery under Arbitrary Power . . . the People . . . absolved from any farther Obedience . . . have a Right to resume their original Liberty."* This is the People's Right of Revolution.

Who was the audience for the Declaration?

The Declaration of Independence was intended for three audiences: the American people, King George and the British Parliament, and the world's nations. It was to motivate as many Americans as possible to join the Revolution, tell the British that America was serious, and recruit potential allies.

The Revolution needed broad support among the American people and international allies. For Americans, the fight was to be for eternal and universal values. To gain allies and support in the international community Americans had to be independent of the British Empire. Without independence there was no hope of help from other countries.

The Declaration of Independence meant to arouse the people to revolt, give believability to America's few friends in the British Parliament, and gain international allies. It was successful in every respect.

The final audience would be future Americans. The Declaration's eternal and universal values continue to speak to us.

Why was there a list of grievances against King George?

Thomas Jefferson, primary author of The Declaration of Independence, was a lawyer. Jefferson patterned the Declaration like a complaint in a court case. There is a statement of law, a list of violations of law and the proper remedy for those violations.

Jefferson stated the law of natural rights, government purpose and the consent of the governed. The list of grievances showed how King George broke the law.

Jefferson then stated the remedy for the King's violations: "these United Colonies are, and of Right ought to be Free and Independent States; that they are Absolved from all Allegiance to the British Crown, and that all political connection between them and the State of Great Britain, is and ought to be totally dissolved . . ."

The list of grievances explained to the American people, the British government and the international community the reasons for American Independence. The list also served the future generations of Americans in listing government action that is intolerable.

Article I: The Congress, Volume Two

Although the federal government was separated into three "co-equal" branches of government, the Founders considered the Congress to be "first among equals." That is why the Constitution's first article is devoted to the Congress, its powers and the limits on those powers.

What are legislative powers?
To the Founders, legislative power was the power to make laws that apply equally to all members of society. The Constitution's Article I, Section 1 states, *"All legislative Powers herein granted shall be vested in a Congress of the United States."*

This legislative power is the authority to make laws and to amend or repeal them. Congress is the branch of government that is charged with making laws. These laws include the levying and collection of taxes, and spending the revenue generated by those taxes.

The Constitution says all powers to make law are granted to Congress. The Constitution does not grant Congress power to allow others to make law. The constitutional principle of a representative republic is violated when Congress grants power to unelected agents of the executive branch to make rules that are for all practical purposes law.

There are federal agencies from FDA, OSHA, EPA, IRS and more that issue "regulations" that control the activities of Americans. These regulations are "laws" and an exercise of the legislative power outside the Constitution.

Why are House members elected for only two years?

At the 1787 constitutional convention there were two schools of thought. In the colonies and newly formed states, the tradition had been to elect legislators every year. Many delegates thought that would be the best for the new government as well. There were others who felt given the size of the country and state of travel and communications in 1787 a three year term would be best. Ultimately the two-year term of office for members of the House of Representatives was a compromise between those who preferred the three year term and those favoring yearly elections.

The House of Representatives was meant to be that part of government closest and most responsive to the people. Short House terms were essential to meet that purpose. The two-year term was practical as well. Presidential and senatorial terms had an even number of years. A two-year House term allowed for holding elections for different offices at the same time.

What does the term "impeachment" mean?

To impeach is to accuse a public official of misconduct in office. Impeachment is saying there is a reason to remove a person from office. It is the first step in a process that *may* remove someone from office. After impeachment a trial takes place to determine if the person is guilty of the misconduct alleged in the articles of impeachment.

The Constitution's Article I gives the power of impeachment of federal officials to the House of Representatives: "*The House of Representatives... shall have the sole power of impeachment.*" That means the House decides (like a grand jury in a criminal case) if there is reason to believe that an official has committed an impeachable offense.

The Constitution's Article II, Section 4 defines an impeachable offense as: "*... treason, bribery, or other high crimes and misdemeanors.*"

This power extends to all officials of the executive and judicial branches, including the president. A majority of the members of the House of Representatives must vote to initiate charges to impeach a federal official.

Why do Senators serve for six years?

The Constitution's Framers understood the necessity for regular elections to keep the government responsive to the people. It was just as important to provide for continuity and stability in the government. Senators were given longer terms to meet the needs of continuity and steadiness.

The citizen politician envisioned by the Framers meant that there would be regular turnover in the legislature. The longer Senate terms meant that even with significant turnover there would be experience or "institutional memory" in the legislature. They did not foresee the career politicians whose time in the legislature would span decades, as has become the reality in the twenty-first century.

The idea was that politicians with some legislative tenure serving together with the more recently elected would maintain a more efficient operation.

Is the Vice-President a member of the legislative branch or the executive branch?

The Constitution's Article I defines the legislative branch. Article I includes the job of the vice-president: "*The Vice President of the United States shall be President of the Senate, but shall have no Vote, unless they be equally divided.*" Besides replacing a president who dies or is unable to serve, the vice-president's only constitutional duties are to preside over the Senate and cast tiebreaking votes. These duties make the vice-president part of the Congress.

The Constitution is very quiet on the job of vice-president and gives no executive authority. Three amendments over a period of 175+ years were needed to clarify even the detail of vice-presidential succession.

Breaking ties does not sound like much, but vice-presidents have voted to break Senate ties 244 times. As far as executive responsibilities, a vice-president only has such duties as the president sees fit to give him. Is the job legislative or executive? You be the judge.

Why must bills for raising revenue be started in the House of Representatives?

The most fundamental power of government and the greatest threat to liberty and natural rights is the power to tax. Considering the taxation abuses under the British kings and Parliament, the Constitution's drafters wanted citizens to have the closest possible eye on taxes. Members of the House of Representatives are elected to short two year terms from local districts and are the government officials nearest to the people. The Senate's members serve longer six-year terms and before the Seventeenth Amendment were chosen by state legislatures not by voters. Even today, though chosen by direct elections, the longer Senate terms and serving an entire state, make Senators less connected to voters.

To provide that the part of government closest to the people would be responsible for taxation, the Constitution's Article I, Section 7, Clause 1, known as the "Origination Clause" provides:

> "*All bills for raising revenue shall originate in the House of Representatives; but the Senate may propose or concur with amendments as on other Bills.*"

If taxes are to be imposed, the Constitution requires they start in the House of Representatives.

When a majority of both Houses of Congress agree on a bill, does it become a law?

In short, not unless the president signs it or a supermajority of Congress passes it over the president's objection. The Constitution mixes some powers among the branches. Article I is devoted to legislative power, but it also gives the president a role in the "making of law." Article I Section 7 provides: "*Every Bill which shall have passed the House of Representatives and the Senate, shall, before it become a Law, be presented to the President of the United States: If he approve he shall sign it, but if not he shall return it with his Objections . . .*"

This is referred to as The Presentment Clause. This provision protects the president's veto power. It also defines the only way in which a federal law is passed: all bills must pass both Houses of Congress and be subject to the President's veto. This is the constitutionally stated method for the creation of a law.

The Presentment Clause might also be properly called The Lawmaking Clause.

What are enumerated powers?

The federal government possesses powers that are specifically defined in the Constitution. These are sometimes referred to as delegated or expressed powers, but typically they are identified as "enumerated powers." The premise of the Constitution is that the federal government is limited to those powers and can do no more than the Constitution allows.

The enumerated powers are found in Article I, Section 8 of the US Constitution, which defines the legislative authority of Congress. That these powers are a limited list is reinforced by the Tenth Amendment which provides: "*The powers not delegated to the United States by the Constitution, nor prohibited by it to the States, are reserved to the States respectively, or to the people.*"

These limits were considered key to maintaining the liberty of the people.

What is the power of Congress to regulate "commerce"?

The Commerce Clause is one of the enumerated powers in Article I, Section 8 of the Constitution. It grants the power "*to regulate commerce with foreign nations, and among the several states, and with the Indian tribes.*"

Trade restrictions between the states during the time of the Articles of Confederation before the Constitution were among the reasons the Articles failed and the Constitution was needed. The Commerce Clause gave Congress the power to address these problems.

For over 150 years the Supreme Court generally saw the Constitution as a limit on Congress's authority. In 1942, that changed with the case of *Wickard v. Filburn*. The Supreme Court ruled that a farmer growing wheat for his own use was part of interstate commerce and could be regulated by Congress.

Once the Supreme Court allowed Congress to fine farmer Roscoe Filburn for growing wheat that he would never sell to anyone, there were few real constitutional limits left on federal power. This changed the meaning of the Constitution dramatically as interpreted by the Supreme Court and was at odds with the concept of a limited government and maximum freedom.

What is the power to declare war?

The Constitution's Article I, Section 8, Clause 11 known as the *War Powers Clause*, confers upon Congress the power to declare war, with the following phrase:

> *"To declare War, grant Letters of Marque and Reprisal, and make Rules concerning Captures on Land and Water;"*

There have been only five formal declarations of war by Congress in US history: The War of 1812, The Mexican-American War, The Spanish-American War, World War I and World War II. Those declarations were quite clear and named eleven nations with whom the United States was at war.

The Constitution does not require Congress to use any particular words to declare war. The country has been at war frequently other than the formally declared conflicts. The lack of an official declaration has not historically inhibited a president from committing forces to military action.

The controversial War Powers Act of 1973, passed over President Nixon's veto, is a congressional effort to assert its control over executive military action. Presidents have taken the position that the Act is unconstitutional.

Article II: The President, Volume Two

The United States had just fought a revolution to free itself from the tyranny of King George. Thomas Paine's *Common Sense* had motivated many to participate in the war against the monarchy. The Constitution's creation of the presidency was a delicate issue.

What does it mean to be Commander-in-Chief?

The Constitution's Article II Section 2 contains the Commander-in-Chief clause: "[t]he President shall be Commander in Chief of the Army and Navy of the United States, and of the Militia of the several States, when called into the actual Service of the United States."

The president commands the armed forces, but is not a member of the military. It was critical to the Framers that a civilian be in control of the military. Civilian authority over the military was viewed as a protection against a military takeover of the country.

The powers of Congress enhance the control of civilians over the military. The Constitution gives Congress the authority to declare war and to control the funding for military operations. These are also checks on the Commander-in-Chief.

Despite these checks presidents claim extensive power from the Commander-in-Chief Clause. Congress, stressing that the Framers made the president Commander-in-Chief to preserve civilian authority over the military, tends to work to restrict the president's power.

Does the president appoint all government officials?

No. The Constitution's Article II, Section 2, Clause 2 is the Appointments Clause and empowers the president to appoint *"with the Advice and Consent of the Senate ... Ambassadors, other public Ministers and Consuls, Judges of the supreme Court, and all other Officers of the United States."*

Lower-level officials may be appointed without the advice and consent process, since *"the Congress may by Law vest the Appointment of such inferior Officers, as they think proper, in the President alone, in the Courts of Law, or in the Heads of Departments."*

The Appointments Clause divides federal officers into two classes: major officers, whose appointments must be made by the president and confirmed by the Senate; and lesser officers, whose appointment Congress may allow to be made by the president or other officials without Senate consent. Congress may create other offices that are not filled by presidential appointment, but by members of the judiciary or designated members of the executive branch. Not every government official is appointed by the president. Allowing judges to appoint other officers of the judicial branch is in keeping with the idea of "separation of powers."

Why is there a State of the Union Address?

The Constitution's Article II, Section 3, Clause 1 says that the President *"shall from time to time give to the Congress Information of the State of the Union, and recommend to their Consideration such Measures as he shall judge necessary and expedient."*

The phrase *"from time to time"* does not impose an obligation on the president to provide Congress information annually. George Washington began the annual tradition with the first presidential address to Congress on January 8, 1790. The president need not address the Congress in person to fulfill the constitutional duty. From 1801 until

1913, the president's "annual message" was sent as a written report. In 1913 Woodrow Wilson resumed the practice of a personal speech and in the 100 years since, only in 1981 was the president's message not delivered to Congress in person. In 1934, Franklin Roosevelt referred to the "state of the union" in his message. By 1947, the president's annual report became known as the State of the Union address.

What does it mean that the laws be faithfully executed?
The Constitution's Article II, Section 3 requires the President to *"take Care that the Laws be faithfully executed."* The Constitution does not command the president to personally execute the laws. He may delegate the execution of the law to others, but the duty to see that the execution is faithful is the president's alone.

The president cannot suspend laws. He may not favor proposed bills over properly enacted laws. He cannot favor political supporters or punish political opponents in his execution of the laws.

English kings had asserted authority to suspend laws unilaterally. The Framers explicitly precluded that practice, and such power is denied to the president.

The president must enforce all constitutionally valid acts of Congress, even if he disagrees with them. The Congress has appropriations, impeachment and other powers over the president if he is unfaithful in his execution of the law.

Why is there a specific presidential oath of office?
All federal, state and local officials take an oath to the Constitution, but the presidential oath is the only oath explicitly written into the Constitution. This was because the powerful American presidency was unlike any office in history.

The office of the president was devised to possess particular attributes: discretion, vitality, secrecy, promptness, and responsiveness. The Framers believed the country's presidency needed such qualities to be effective, particularly in a time of crisis. The office was created with these thoughts in mind.

The president was granted great power, but the Constitution restrains that power. The president must work within those restraints.

The specific oath is designed to call the president's attention to the constitutional limits on his power. Before taking office the president swears to exercise his power within constitutional limitations. The following oath is to remind him he is not a king:

> *I do solemnly swear (or affirm) that I will faithfully execute the Office of President of the United States, and will to the best of my Ability, preserve, protect and defend the Constitution of the United States.*

Article III: The Judiciary Volume Two

Over the 226+ years since the Constitution was adopted, the branch that was given the least attention in the Constitution has indeed become a co-equal part of the federal government. The specific power of the Supreme Court provided by the Constitution was not broad, and the Constitution allows the Congress to define and limit the Court further. However, the Court gets to say what the law means. The Supreme Court has said that the law means it is very powerful.

Does the Constitution give the courts power to declare a law unconstitutional?

The power to declare a law unconstitutional is not mentioned in the Constitution. Article III, which defines court authority, provides: "*The judicial Power shall extend to all Cases . . . arising under this Constitution.*" Article VI commands that: "*This Constitution . . . shall be the supreme Law of the Land.*"

The question arises: What's a judge to do when another law conflicts with the Constitution? John Marshall answered that question in *Marbury v. Madison*:

... if a law be in opposition to the Constitution ... so that the Court must either decide ... conformably to the law, disregarding the Constitution, or conformably to the Constitution, disregarding the law ... the Constitution is superior to any ordinary act of the legislature, the Constitution, and not such ordinary act, must govern ...

The Constitution did not explicitly give courts the power to declare laws unconstitutional. It did give the power to decide constitutional cases and denote the Constitution as the supreme law. With that combination, the court's power, now known as judicial review, simply makes sense.

Why are federal judges appointed for life?

Judges are appointed for life to avoid having them subject to the pressures of current political and social events. If there was a change of judges every time the party in power changed, then they would make decisions not based upon the law, but rather by the desire to preserve their jobs. The life terms permit judges to be free from public or political forces in deciding cases.

The founders wanted to separate the judges from politics so they would be impartial in rendering their judgments without the concern of retribution for an unpopular verdict.

The lifetime appointment of judges also guarantees the separation of powers between the branches. Judges would not owe their continued employment to the presidents that appointed them or the Senators that conferred their consent.

The Constitution's Article III of the Constitution guarantees both a judge's job and salary to insure an independent judicial branch.

What is the only crime defined in the Constitution?

Treason is the only crime defined in the Constitution. Article III, Section 3 provides that *"Treason against the United States, shall consist only in levying War against them, or in adhering to their Enemies, giving them Aid and Comfort."*

The crime of treason was made constitutional to make it specific and not subject to change by Congress and used for politics. The Framers knew the British government had misused the charge against political foes.

During the ratification debates the Constitution's supporters made clear that treason's limited definition would protect ordinary political practices from tyrannical prosecutions.

In English law, for a long time before the Revolution, just thinking about the king's death (known as "compassing") was treason. The charge was used freely against political adversaries and the danger of an arrest for treason due to mere criticism of the government could chill most opposition.

Paraphrasing Ben Franklin, the charge of treason was the excuse the winners used to hang the losers. That would not be the case in the American republic.

Article IV: State Relations

- Article IV governs the relationships among **THE STATES**. Under the Articles of Confederation, the **STATES** treated one another like independent sovereign nations, but under the Constitution, **THE STATES** had to respect one another's **COURT DECISIONS and LAWS**.

Article IV: Government Relations, Volume Two

The Constitution created a dual system of government that was unique in world history with different governments responsible for different subjects over the same territory. This was American Federalism, and the Constitution includes many details of how the federal government would relate to the states and how the states would relate to each other. Article IV addresses many of these issues. The goal was to have both levels of government able to govern, and yet to be a check on each other to protect the people's liberty.

The Constitution requires the states to have what form of government?

Every state in the union must be a republic. This command is in the Constitution's Guarantee Clause of Article IV which requires the United States to "... *guarantee to every State in this Union a Republican Form of Government ...*" This means a government without a king, accountable to the people and governed by the "rule of law." States would have no kings, elections for government representatives and an established law applied equally to all citizens. This is the essence of a republic.

For a State to be admitted to the Union, it must establish a republican government. The Founders wanted no kings of states nor the "mobocracy" that comes with "direct democracy." A "republican form of government" protects the rights of all citizens, not just those of a momentary majority. Protecting republican government throughout the country means protecting republican government in each state.

James Madison made this clear in Federalist No. 10.

Does the federal government have an obligation to the states in case of invasion?

In the Constitution the federal government also guarantees to the States that it *"shall protect each of them against Invasion . . ."*

At a minimum it is the federal government's duty to protect States from foreign invasion, with military force if needed. This clause obligates the federal government to secure the country's borders. This guarantee is a part of a general constitutional goal, that although the United States may share power with the states internally, the country is to have a single foreign policy speak with one voice to the outside world. The federal government's obligation to provide border security is required by the Constitution.

Which government is primarily responsible for addressing issues of violence within the borders of a state?

The states are primarily responsible for violence within their borders. The last provision of the Guarantee Clause directs the federal government to protect each state: ". . . on Application of the Legislature, or of the Executive (when the Legislature cannot be convened), against domestic Violence.

This is important because it authorizes the legislature of each state (or the executive, if the legislature cannot be assembled in time) to request federal help with riots or other violence.

The message is that without a state request for federal help for violence within its borders, the federal government may not legally dispatch troops (or federalize the National Guard) to address violence within a state. Congress's responsibility for quelling domestic violence is secondary to the states. Federal authority exists only when a state asks for help. The Constitution's presumption is that absent a state invitation, the central government cannot send in the army to "insure domestic tranquility." This is consistent with the Founding view that a standing army was a threat to liberty.

Article V

The Congress, whenever two thirds of both houses shall deem it necessary, shall propose amendments to this Constitution, or, on the application of the legislatures of two thirds of the several states, shall call a convention for proposing amendments, which, in either case, shall be valid to all intents and purposes, as part of this Constitution, when ratified by the legislatures of three fourths of the several states, or by conventions in three fourths thereof, as the one or the other mode of ratification may be proposed by the Congress; provided that no amendment which may be made prior to the year one thousand eight hundred and eight shall in any manner affect the first and fourth clauses in the ninth section of the first article; and that no state, without its consent, shall be deprived of its equal suffrage in the Senate.

Article V: Amendments

While the Framers gave careful consideration to constructing the government, they had the wisdom to know they could not provide for every possibility or for every change the future would bring. Understanding this, Article V was included to allow for amending or changing the Constitution.

Can the Constitution be changed?

The Constitution can be changed through amendments.

The Founding Fathers wanted a Constitution that could stand the test of time. They knew that changing circumstances would bring different issues, challenges and a need to alter the US government's charter and included an amendment process. The Constitution's Article V defines this process:

> *The Congress, whenever two-thirds of both Houses shall deem it necessary, shall propose Amendments to this Constitution, or, on*

the Application of the Legislatures of two thirds of the several States,
shall call a Convention for proposing Amendments, which, in ei-
ther Case, shall be valid, to all Intents and Purposes, as Part of
this Constitution, when ratified by the Legislatures of three fourths
of the several States, or by conventions in three fourths thereof, as
the one or the other Mode of Ratification may be proposed by the
Congress.

How are amendments to the Constitution proposed?

The Constitution's Article V provides two methods to propose amendments. The first, and only method ever used, is for two-thirds of each
House of Congress to propose an Amendment and send it to the States
for ratification.

The second method is for two-thirds of the State legislatures to apply to Congress to call a Convention for the proposing of Amendments.
Article V provides that *"Congress shall"* call the convention once ⅔ of
the states have requested a convention. This method has never been
used.

Over time, when an Amendment Convention has appeared likely,
Congress has acted to propose amendments to avoid such a convention. There are strong movements currently to have a convention for
amendments Congress refuses to propose related to a balanced bud-
get and term limits for members of Congress.

How do amendments to the Constitution become effective?

Proposed amendments become effective when "ratified" or approved
by three-fourths of the states.

The Constitution's Article V about amendments provides for two
methods of ratifying amendments that have been proposed to the
states. The first, ratification by three-fourths of the State legislatures,
has been used for twenty-six of the twenty-seven amendments to the
Constitution.

The second method for ratification is by state ratification conventions. These conventions are made up of delegates elected by the
people for the single purpose of deciding whether or not to ratify a
particular amendment. To be ratified a proposed amendment needs

approval of three-fourths of the state conventions. This method has been used once, for the Twenty-First Amendment, repealing the Eighteenth Amendment and Prohibition.

Many members of the state legislatures still supported Prohibition and Congress thought repeal of Prohibition might fail if left to the legislatures, that's why the convention method was selected to ratify the Twenty-First Amendment.

Are there limits on the power to amend the Constitution?

Article V prohibited certain amendments to the Constitution:

> *Provided that no Amendment which may be made prior to the Year One thousand eight hundred and eight shall in any Manner affect the first and fourth Clauses in the Ninth Section of the first Article; and that no State, without its Consent, shall be deprived of its equal Suffrage in the Senate.*

Constitutional amendments to limit congressional power to ban the importation of slaves prior to 1808 and the power to impose direct taxes prior to a national census were prohibited. Those two provisions expired and Congress did prohibit the importation of slaves and imposed direct taxes.

There still cannot be a constitutional amendment to reduce a State's vote in the Senate. All states must have two Senators and two votes.

Is it difficult to amend the Constitution?

Yes. The process to build a large national consensus to change the Constitution was made purposefully difficult. While Article V provided a process for amendments the Constitution was to hold a special place in American law and was not to be changed easily. Amendments require majorities of ⅔ in the House and Senate or ⅔ of the states to petition to be proposed. Ratification requires three-fourths of the states.

The Constitution is to have continuity and not be easily changed by short-term sentiment. Congress has sent only thirty-three amendments to the states for ratification, and only twenty-seven have passed, despite thousands of proposals. Of the twenty-seven that have been ratified, the first ten, known as the Bill of Rights, were ratified just four years after the Constitution was proposed. The next seventeen were added over a period of more than 200 years. The Twenty-Seventh Amendment, first proposed in 1789 took over 200 years to be ratified. It is a difficult process.

Can the Supreme Court change the Constitution?

The Court cannot "change" the Constitution, though through history it has changed its understanding of what the words mean. The Article V amendment process was made difficult to ensure widespread agreement for changing the Constitution. Drastic changes by the court without an actual amendment can be the source of significant political conflict because it short circuited the amendment process.

The Supreme Court has assumed the power of final interpreter of the Constitution's words, and retains the power to overrule its own previous decisions. In overruling itself on constitutional questions the Supreme Court changes the way the document is read and the effect can be the same as an amendment, though the Constitution's words have not changed. Such power was not explicitly granted in Article III.

A Supreme Court decision can be overruled by a constitutional amendment. This has clearly happened three times. The Eleventh, Fourteenth and Sixteenth Amendments overruled Supreme Court decisions.

Why are there provisions for changing the Constitution outside of Congress?

The states have never used a power granted to them to amend the Constitution provided in Article V. This provision exists so that states can independently propose and adopt amendments with the participation of Congress.

The Framers were concerned that if the only power to propose amendments belonged to Congress, the federal government would never do anything that might limit its own power. The Constitution's drafters and ratifiers required Congress to call a convention if the states requested it and the states could act without the participation of Congress.

> *If two thirds of those legislatures require it, Congress must call a general convention, even though they dislike the proposed amendments, and if three fourths of the state legislatures or conventions approve such proposed amendments, they become an actual and binding part of the constitution, without any possible interference of Congress.*
>
> Trench Coxe, June 11, 1788.

This ability of the states to change the Constitution was seen as a check on federal power and of crucial importance in the ratification of the Constitution.

Is the Amendment process related to the Declaration of Independence?

The Declaration of Independence declares: *"whenever any Form of Government becomes destructive of these ends, it is the Right of the People to alter or to abolish it . . ."* This means if government fails in its purpose of securing the people's inalienable rights of life, liberty and the pursuit of happiness, the people have a right to alter or abolish it. This is a statement of the Right of Revolution, but with a focus on "alter," it is the Right of Amendment.

A constitution that contained no amendment process would be a document that could not be altered. This would leave the people with no recourse but to violently abolish the government. One of the most important features of the Constitution is that it can be altered, expanded or contracted without replacing the entire document and without a violent revolution.

The inclusion of an amendment process reveals another connection between the Declaration of Independence and the Constitution that is often overlooked.

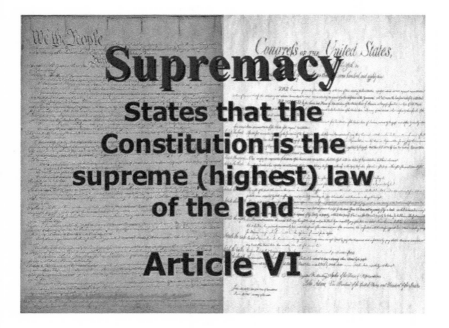

Supremacy

States that the Constitution is the supreme (highest) law of the land

Article VI

Article VI: Debts, Oaths and the Supremacy Clause

This Constitution, and the Laws of the United States which shall be made in pursuance thereof; and all treaties made, or which shall be made, under the authority of the United States, shall be the supreme law of the land ... anything in the constitution or laws of any state to the contrary notwithstanding.

A major failure of the Articles of Confederation was the inability of the Confederation Congress to enforce its "resolutions." The Confederation Congress did not truly pass laws, but rather made requests of the states. To correct this problem, the Constitution became the highest law in the country, or the Supreme Law of the Land. To emphasize the Constitution's supremacy, all government officials whether federal, state or local were required to take an oath to support the Constitution.

Did the Constitution provide for payment of debts incurred by earlier governments?

The United States had borrowed millions of dollars to finance the revolution. The United States borrowed much of this money from the Dutch and French. The foreign creditors needed assurance that a change in government would not affect the debts owed to them. The Constitution's Article VI provided this assurance:

All Debts contracted and Engagements entered into, before the Adoption of this Constitution, shall be as valid against the United States under this Constitution, as under the Confederation.

For the United States to be accepted by the other countries of the world, the new government had to be creditworthy. This constitutional commitment to honoring the country's international debts contributed to its growth into the world's premiere economic power.

What was an oath when the Constitution was written?

At the time of the Founding an oath taker was understood to make two promises. One was to the community as a juror, witness or office holder. The other was to God. It was believed that while a person might lie to the community, he would be less likely to lie to God and risk His wrath for all eternity. This was an extra assurance of the oath taker's truthfulness. The word "oath" and phrase "solemnly swear" included the promise to God. The Constitution requires oaths in several places, yet allows for an affirmation instead of an oath. This may be because Quakers were important in the Founding and their objections have Biblical roots in James 5:12: *"But above all things, my brethren, swear not, neither by heaven, neither by the earth . . . lest ye fall into condemnation."*

In modern times, though we have lost the consensus of sanctity, certain promises said out loud in ceremonial or judicial proceedings are referred to as oaths.

Who is required to take an oath by the Constitution and why?

Taking of an oath was very serious business in the eighteenth century, and the Founders wanted to create a "national government." The traditional loyalty of Americans had been to their state. Before Independence, people referred to Massachusetts or Virginia as their home "country." Creating loyalty to the Union was critical to creating a "nation."

The Constitution's oath requirements were part of creating a nation. Not only were oaths supporting the Constitution required of the president and other federal office holders, but Article VI required oaths of state and local officials as well:

The Senators and Representatives before mentioned, and the Members of the several State Legislatures, and all executive and

judicial Officers, both of the United States and of the several States,
shall be bound by Oath or Affirmation, to support this Constitution;
but no religious Test shall ever be required as a Qualification to any
Office or public Trust under the United States.

All government officials across the United States take an oath of
office and swear to support the Constitution. This act reminds every
official from dog catcher to president that they have constitutional
obligations.

What is the Supremacy Clause?

The Constitution's Article VI contains the Supremacy Clause, providing that the Constitution, laws passed by Congress and treaties of the
United States are the supreme law of the land. The Supremacy Clause
establishes an order of law in the United States, to be followed by all
judges, state or federal. The Constitution mandates:

This Constitution, and the Laws of the United States which shall be
made in Pursuance thereof; and all Treaties made, or which shall
be made, under the Authority of the United States, shall be the su-
preme Law of the Land; and the Judges in every State shall be bound
thereby, any Thing in the Constitution or Laws of any State to the
contrary notwithstanding.

If Congress passes a law under a power granted in Article I, then
state law must defer. This constitutional mandate is called preemption.

While the Constitution is the Supreme Law of the Land, is there an order of importance of other laws in the United States?

The Constitution's Supremacy Clause lists four classes of law in a specific order. The order of listing is as follows:

- **The Constitution** is listed first and therefore is supreme over
  other laws of the land.
- **Laws** passed *pursuant* to the Constitution are listed second.
  As Alexander Hamilton wrote in Federalist No. 33, laws not

authorized by the Constitution: "*. . . would not be the supreme law of the land, but a usurpation of power not granted by the Constitution . . .*"

- **Treaties** made *under the authority of the United States* are listed third. Since treaties are listed third, any changes they may require in other laws, must be passed by the Senate and House and signed by the President.
- **State constitutions and laws** are listed fourth and state judges are required to follow federal law when state and federal law are in conflict.

This is part of the complex web of law that governs our lives.

Are there areas of law when federal law is not more important than state law?

The federal government and each of the fifty states have their own constitutions. The US Constitution and the state constitutions are sets of rules for government, defining the organization, and enumerating government's powers, limits and functions.

By virtue of its Supremacy Clause, the US Constitution is the "supreme law of the land." However, in some instances, because of the Tenth Amendment, which reserves powers to the states not granted to the federal government by the Constitution, state constitutions and laws have more force and effect in specific areas. The states principally control matters such as local criminal law, land law, contract law, and family law. Those are among the powers recognized as reserved to the people by the Tenth Amendment. This division of "subject matter jurisdiction" between government units in the same territory is the essence of American Federalism and serves as another protection for the people's liberty.

Article VII: Ratification

State	Date	Votes in Favor–Against
Delaware	December 8, 1787	30 – 9
Pennsylvania	December 12, 1787	46 – 23
New Jersey	December 18, 1787	38 – 0
Georgia	January 2, 1788	26 – 0
Connecticut	January 9, 1788	128 – 40
Massachusetts	February 16, 1788	187 – 168
Maryland	April 26, 1788	63 – 11
South Carolina	May 23, 1788	149 – 73
New Hampshire	June 21, 1788	57 – 47
Virginia	June 25, 1788	89 – 79
New York	July 26, 1788	30 – 27
North Carolina	November 21, 1789	194 – 77
Rhode Island	May 29, 1790	34 – 32

The Constitution went into effect through a process of Ratification. This process is set forth in Article VII. The process served several purposes. One of the most important was to keep faith with a principle of the Declaration of Independence: obtaining the consent of the governed.

Did the adoption of the Constitution maintain the values of the Declaration of Independence?

The Declaration of Independence required the "consent of the governed" for a government to be legitimate. The Articles of Confederation had been an agreement among the states. The Constitution would be different from the Articles of Confederation. The Constitution was to create a government established by the people. To be consistent with the Declaration, the Constitution had to include a system for obtaining the people's consent.

State ratifying conventions were selected as a method to secure the consent of the people. Through the convention debates the people would learn about the proposed new government. The Constitution's advocates and adversaries would have the chance to discuss the Constitution in public.

These state conventions had delegates elected for a single purpose: to vote on the Constitution. The convention representatives were chosen specifically to provide the "consent of the governed" for the proposed new government. It was they who decided to accept or reject the Constitution. This process kept faith with the Declaration of Independence.

Was unanimous ratification required for the Constitution to take effect?

The Constitution required only nine of the thirteen states to go into effect in the states that approved. This and the amendment provisions meant a government vastly different from that under the Articles of Confederation. The Articles had required the approval of every state for any action.

To form a single country from thirteen states, no state could hold the power to frustrate the will of the Union. The Constitution's and Article VII ratification provisions did not require the consent of every state.

The Article VII ratification provision reads as follows:

> "*The Ratification of the Conventions of nine States, shall be sufficient for the Establishment of this Constitution between the States so ratifying the Same*"

This requirement of only nine of thirteen states for ratification and ¾ of the States for amendments meant each State gave up significant power. The Constitution required member States to give up power and to accept changes a State might not approve. This meant the States would become a nation rather than an alliance.

Which state ratified first and when was the ratification process complete?

Delaware on December 7, 1787 became the first state to ratify the Constitution, earning its nickname: "The First State." The Constitution became effective when New Hampshire provided the ninth ratification on June 21, 1788. Government under the Constitution began in March 1789.

The Declaration of Independence set forth the legal authority to establish the United States. Natural Law was the organizing principle. A core principle of Natural Law is that people agree to limits on certain natural rights in order to gain the benefits of a civil society. The Article VII ratification process was to obtain the consent of the people consistent with founding principles. The people's consent to establish the Constitution continued adherence to the Natural Law principles giving legitimacy to the government.

Was ratification of the Constitution legal?

The Constitution's ratification process raises an interesting historical legal question. The Articles of Confederation required unanimous approval to change, but the Constitution did not require unanimity to go into effect. On June 21, 1788 New Hampshire became the ninth state to ratify the Constitution and the document became effective pursuant to Article VII.

It was not until Rhode Island's May 29, 1790 ratification that there was the unanimous approval of the States required to change the Articles. The Constitution, by its terms was effective with New Hampshire's ratification nearly two years earlier. The question: Did the United States have two separate governments during the time between New Hampshire's ratification and Rhode Island's?

Bill of Rights
Congress OF THE United
begun and held at the City of New York, on
Wednesday the fourth of March, one thousand seven hundred and

The Bill of Rights, Volume Two

The first ten amendments have become known as the Bill of Rights. While these amendments were changes to the originally ratified Constitution, supporters of the Constitution had promised to add a Bill of Rights during the debates about whether the document should be adopted. The supporters' promises were kept by the First Congress. This section is an introduction to the Bill of Rights as a whole. Volume III will be devoted to all twenty-seven amendments that have been to date adopted.

Does the Bill of Rights grant rights to Americans?
The Bill of Rights does not grant the inalienable rights referred to in the Declaration of Independence. These rights already belong to every human being at birth. On the other hand, there are rights contained in the Bill of Rights that might be called "procedural rights." These rights grew out of the American desire to limit government. "Procedural rights" are protections for the inalienable natural rights mentioned in the Declaration of Independence.

There are a group of rights that the Bill of Rights specifically withdraws from government the authority to interfere with. It is significant that the first phrase in the Bill of Rights is "*Congress shall make no law . . .*" This clearly indicates limits on government power.

The Bill of Rights recognizes the natural rights of life, liberty and property. Government is specifically limited in the areas of religion, speech, free press, free assembly, and the right to keep and bear arms to protect those natural rights. Other rights, such as a speedy trial, to remain silent, to have an attorney and more are procedural protections for our natural rights.

Why was a Bill of Rights added to the Constitution?
The Constitutional Convention finished its work in September 1787. The ratification process followed, and during that process opposition arose because the proposed Constitution contained no Bill of Rights. The Constitution's supporters promised to add one after ratification.

James Madison proposed nineteen amendments to the First Congress. Congress, by joint resolution, sent twelve of these amendments to the states on September 25, 1789.

On December 15, 1791, with Virginia's ratification, ten of the proposed amendments became part of the Constitution and known as the Bill of Rights.

The first two proposed amendments were not ratified. One of those two, an amendment that placed limits on when Congress could alter the pay of congressmen and Senators, was ratified more than 200 years later, becoming the Twenty-Seventh Amendment. The Constitution's supporters during the ratification debates and candidates during the first congressional elections had promised to add a Bill of Rights. The supporters of the Constitution and winners of the first congressional elections kept that promise.

How did James Madison choose the amendment proposals he offered when drafting a suggested Bill of Rights?
The Constitutional Convention finished its work on September 17, 1787. The Constitution's Article VII provided that the Constitution would go into effect when nine of the thirteen states had ratified the document. Ratification was by no means assured. There were groups known as Federalists that favored ratification and the Anti-Federalists who opposed the Constitution.

Among the Anti-Federalist arguments against the Constitution was the lack of specific protections from the federal government for citizens of their most important natural rights. To secure votes for ratification, the Constitution's supporters promised amendments to address the lack of detailed protections for natural rights.

New York, Virginia and others included recommendations for amendments attached to their resolutions of ratification. James

Madison used these recommendations for guidance in the proposals he offered to the First Congress as it began the work of keeping the promise to add a Bill of Rights.

Was the federal government limited in its conduct by the enumeration of powers?

The US Constitution grants enumerated powers to the central government. The Constitution's supporters, the Federalists, believed a specific list of powers limited the government to those powers. This idea is based upon a rule for interpreting legal documents: "*the express mention of one thing excludes all others.*"

The Anti-Federalists didn't wish to leave protection of inalienable natural rights to a legal saying. These concerns resulted in the first ten amendments, the Bill of Rights. As an example: the First Amendment restricts the federal government actions in the areas related to our natural rights:

> *Congress shall make no law respecting an establishment of religion, or prohibiting the free exercise thereof; or abridging the freedom of speech, or of the press; or the right of the people peaceably to assemble, and to petition the Government for a redress of grievances.*

The Bill of Rights was the final act of creating the original Constitution. It had been promised during ratification and the First Congress made good on that promise.

DAVID J. SHESTOKAS

CONSTITUTIONAL SOUND BITES

VOLUME THREE
THE BILL OF RIGHTS

TO THE ANTI-FEDERALISTS, WITHOUT WHOSE DEDICATION
TO LIBERTY IT IS LIKELY THERE WOULD HAVE BEEN
NO BILL OF RIGHTS AND TO JAMES MADISON AND
THE MEMBERS OF THE FIRST CONGRESS WHO KEPT
THE PROMISE MADE TO ADD A BILL OF RIGHTS.

CONSTITUTIONAL SOUND BITES

VOLUME THREE

DAVID J. SHESTOKAS

CONSTITUTIONALLY SPEAKING
Lemont, IL

Introduction, Volume Three

Every word of the Constitution decides a question between power and liberty...

James Madison, Father of the Bill of Rights

This statement is true throughout the Constitution, but the first ten amendments, known as the Bill of Rights are the words most directly devoted to limiting power and protecting liberty. This third volume of the *Constitutional Sound Bites* series is focused on those limits and protections. Like the first two volumes, *Volume Three* gives the reader short "sound bites" on the constitutional topics covered. Each "sound bite" is intended to give the reader an understanding of the history, philosophy or concept addressed by a question that precedes the "sound bite."

This volume opens, as do Volumes One and Two, with chapters entitled Constitutional Considerations and Thoughts on the Declaration of Independence. Constitutional Considerations gives background on history and philosophy that help to understand the rest of the book. Thoughts on the Declaration of Independence emphasizes how the Declaration and the Bill of Rights are directly connected. The connection is key to understanding why there is a Bill of Rights.

Volumes One and Two concentrated on the Original Constitution prior to any amendments. The Bill of Rights, while properly classified as a group of amendments, was actually the last element of the process in the creation of the Constitution and the Founding of America.

After the new Constitution was submitted to the states in 1787 for ratification, several states approved it only after being assured that a bill of rights would be added. Without a promise by the Constitution's supporters during the ratification debates of 1787–89 to add a Bill of Rights there would have been no Constitution. To keep that promise, the First Congress organized under the Constitution proposed twelve amendments on September 25, 1789. By December 15, 1791 ten amendments were ratified by the states, becoming the Bill of Rights.

The Bill of Rights, which represented for James Madison, "... the great rights of mankind" are of critical significance. These amendments were adopted to limit the power of the federal government. When the Fourteenth Amendment was adopted after the Civil War, the power of state governments was also limited by the Bill of Rights. Now all governments in the United States, whether that government is federal, state or local are subject to the Bill of Rights.

Once the Fourteenth Amendment placed constitutional limits on the acts of state governments (*"No State shall make or enforce any law ..."*) another constitutional provision came into play.

Because of the Article VI Supremacy Clause the Constitution trumps all other law in the country. The Supremacy Clause, the Bill of Rights and the Fourteenth Amendment act together to place limits on every act of government in the country. The result is that when a federal, state or local government action, whether a law, rule, or order, clashes with the Bill of Rights, the Bill of Rights wins. This limits the power of government and protects the rights of Americans.

While most government officials attempt to follow the Constitution as they go about their work, many fail to do so. The American founders were aware that this would happen and that is why the Bill of Rights exists: so American citizens can point to the Bill of Rights and require the government to follow the law.

Police may stop someone without the probable cause required by the Fourth Amendment. A local official may deny a permit to hold a political rally violating the Free Speech provisions of the First Amendment. A gun may be confiscated in violation of the Second Amendment. To correct such wrongs, Americans file thousands of lawsuits every year to defend their constitutional rights. The only way for a citizen to know if a right has been violated is to be aware the right exists. The goal of *Constitutional Sound Bites Volume Three* is to increase that awareness.

Often the best way to understand a right is the story of how it came to be in the Bill of Rights, whether as a recognition of the inalienable rights of the Declaration of Independence, or as a "procedural right" to provide protection for the inalienable rights. That's why many of the "sound bites" are brief histories of the rights. Knowledge of the origins provides understanding of why a right is in the Bill and what it is supposed to protect. That knowledge helps to recognize when a right has been violated, and when to take action to protect it.

The message here is protection. The term "inalienable" literally means something that cannot be "legally" taken away. That does not mean that government might not try to interfere with someone's rights to life, liberty and the pursuit of happiness. It means such interference is illegal. It is for all of us to know our rights and not just defend our own rights, but the rights of our fellow citizens. If their rights are infringed, the day will come when our own will be in danger.

Congrefs OF THE United States

begun and held at the City of New York, on
Wednesday the, Fourth of March, one thousand seven hundred and eighty-nine

THE Conventions of a number of the States having at the time of their adopting the Constitution, expressed a desire in order to prevent misconstruction or abuse of its powers, that further declaratory and restrictive clauses should be added: And as extending the ground of public confidence in the Government, will best insure the beneficent ends of its institution.

RESOLVED by the Senate and House of Representatives of the United States of America in Congress assembled, two thirds of both Houses concurring, that the following Articles be proposed to the Legislatures of the several States, as amendments to the Constitution of the United States, all or any of which articles, when ratified by three fourths of the said Legislatures, to be valid to all intents and purposes as part of the said Constitution, viz.

ARTICLES in addition to, and amendment of the Constitution of the United States of America, proposed by Congress, and ratified by the Legislatures of the several States, pursuant to the fifth Article of the original Constitution.

Article the first. After the first enumeration required by the first Article of the Constitution, there shall be one Representative for every thirty thousand, until the number shall amount to one hundred, after which the proportion shall be so regulated by Congress, that there shall be not less than one hundred Representatives, nor less than one Representative for every forty thousand persons, until the number of Representatives shall amount to two hundred, after which the proportion shall be so regulated by Congress, that there shall not be less than two hundred Representatives, nor more than one Representative for every fifty thousand persons.

Article the second. No law varying the compensation for the services of the Senators and Representatives, shall take effect, until an election of Representatives shall have intervened.

Article the third. Congress shall make no law respecting an establishment of religion, or prohibiting the free exercise thereof; or abridging the freedom of speech, or of the press; or the right of the people peaceably to assemble, and to petition the Government for a redress of grievances.

Article the fourth. A well regulated Militia, being necessary to the security of a free State, the right of the people to keep and bear arms, shall not be infringed.

Article the fifth. No Soldier shall, in time of peace be quartered in any house, without the consent of the Owner, nor in time of war, but in a manner to be prescribed by law.

Article the sixth. The right of the people to be secure in their persons, houses, papers, and effects, against unreasonable searches and seizures, shall not be violated, and no warrants shall issue, but upon probable cause, supported by oath or affirmation, and particularly describing the place to be searched, and the persons or things to be seized.

Article the seventh. No person shall be held to answer for a capital, or otherwise infamous crime, unless on a presentment or indictment of a Grand Jury, except in cases arising in the land or naval forces, or in the Militia, when in actual service in time of war or public danger; nor shall any person be subject for the same offence to be twice put in jeopardy of life or limb; nor shall be compelled in any criminal case to be a witness against himself, nor be deprived of life, liberty, or property, without due process of law; nor shall private property be taken for public use, without just compensation.

Article the eighth. In all criminal prosecutions, the accused shall enjoy the right to a speedy and public trial, by an impartial jury of the State and district wherein the crime shall have been committed, which district shall have been previously ascertained by law, and to be informed of the nature and cause of the accusation; to be confronted with the witnesses against him; to have compulsory process for obtaining witnesses in his favor, and to have the Assistance of Counsel for his defence.

Article the ninth. In suits at common law, where the value in controversy shall exceed twenty dollars, the right of trial by jury shall be preserved, and no fact tried by a jury, shall be otherwise re-examined in any Court of the United States, than according to the rules of the common law.

Article the tenth. Excessive bail shall not be required, nor excessive fines imposed, nor cruel and unusual punishments inflicted.

Article the eleventh. The enumeration in the Constitution, of certain rights, shall not be construed to deny or disparage others retained by the people.

Article the twelfth. The powers not delegated to the United States by the Constitution, nor prohibited by it to the States, are reserved to the States respectively, or to the people.

ATTEST.

Frederick Augustus Muhlenberg, Speaker of the House of Representatives,

John Adams, Vice-President of the United States and President of the Senate,

John Beckley, Clerk of the House of Representatives,

Sam. A. Otis, Secretary of the Senate.

Certifyed by John X Callitey Jr D

Constitutional Considerations

Reading the Constitution gets off to a wonderful start with the Preamble's soaring statement of purpose. After that much of it reads like a technical legal document, which it is. It becomes more entertaining when you look for the goals to be achieved with separation of powers, American Federalism or republican principles. This is equally true when considering the Bill of Rights. The first ten amendments are pieces of the jigsaw puzzle that fit together with the unamended Constitution to meet the goals of the Preamble.

This section, Constitutional Considerations, points out some of the puzzle pieces to help see how different aspects of the Constitution fit together to reveal a limited government that provides maximum freedom.

Are Amendments part of the Constitution?
By definition amendments are part of the Constitution when ratified. Article V provides that properly adopted amendments "... *shall be valid to all Intents and Purposes, as Part of this Constitution, when ratified ...*" In the strict legal sense, all twenty-seven amendments are "part" of the Constitution. This misses the true meaning of "The Constitution."

The unamended Constitution was an effort to fulfill the promise and philosophy of the Declaration of Independence and the Constitution's Preamble. Only the "Bill of Rights," among all the amendments since 1789, were added to Constitution to complete the definition of "America" at its founding. The Bill of Rights was the final step of the original process of setting up America.

Amendments Eleven through Twenty-Seven address different subjects for different times. Many, like the Twelfth and Twenty-Fifth, address technical problems. The Civil War Amendments, (Thirteenth, Fourteenth and Fifteenth) resolved an issue the Founders had avoided, slavery. The Eighteenth Amendment, with its Prohibition, restrained liberty contrary to the founding principles. Unlike men, not all amendments are created equal.

Does the Constitution grant the central government power or does it limit power?

The purpose of a constitution is to express in general principles the shared understandings of a people with respect to their government. It defines powers and sets up agencies of government to execute and carry out the principles it formulates. In defining powers, a constitution both confers power and places a limit on the use of that power.

The American government's main source of power is from the Article I list of subjects that Congress can regulate, call enumerated powers. That is how the Constitution confers power.

The Constitution limits the power of the federal government two ways. One limit is the original structure that provided only specific powers and no more. The other way is by explicit limitations found in the Bill of Rights, which begins: "*Congress shall make no law . . .*"

Why does the language of the Declaration of Independence, Constitution and Bill of Rights sound a bit strange?

The Founding Documents would have been well understood by an ordinary, reasonably well informed English speaker in eighteenth century America. At the time the documents explained crucial ideas to the general public. That the general public understood is evidenced by the fact that Americans came together to support the Revolution and the new government. The language was not strange in eighteenth century America.

Thomas Jefferson's goal with the Declaration of Independence was to explain the "common sense" of the matter. The people of the time clearly understood, not only the words, but the ideas since they acted upon the ideas. The language was not strange to them and the ideas should not be strange to us.

The Declaration, the Constitution, and the Bill of Rights all convey the idea that everyone has fundamental rights that governments are created to protect. Those rights include natural rights that are inherent in all people by virtue of their being human. Regardless of the language the ideas live through the centuries.

Throughout the Constitution and Bill of Rights there are references to the "common law." What does this mean?

In medieval England, the law was simply the word of the King, bishop or sheriff, often mixing secular law with liturgical law tracing back to the Ten Commandments. The King appointed judges to serve throughout the kingdom. Early on different judges would decide matters with similar facts differently. In 1154, under King Henry II, judges began returning to London to discuss cases and record their decisions. A system of precedent evolved around the concept of *stare decisis* (Latin for "to stand by decisions").

The judges' recorded decisions would be studied and followed by other judges deciding cases with facts similar to earlier cases. These records of cases became the *common law*. The American colonies were subject to the common law of England. English common law was the earliest law for the United States. It remained in effect as precedent, even after the Constitution was adopted.

Thoughts on the Declaration of Independence

Before his death, Thomas Jefferson left clear instructions about the tombstone to be set up over his grave and the words with which he wanted it to be inscribed:

Here was buried
Thomas Jefferson
Author of the Declaration of American Independence,
Of the Statute of Virginia for religious freedom
& Father of the University of Virginia

The Declaration of Independence not only announced that the colonies were leaving the British Empire. It also stated the new nation's guiding principles. It was unprecedented to found a country based upon a philosophy that started with "all men are created equal." This "self-evident" truth and others expressed in the Declaration are at work in the Constitution. The Bill of Rights, with its specific protections for inalienable rights is a direct descendant of the Declaration of Independence.

What is the relationship of the Declaration of Independence to the Bill of Rights?
The Declaration of Independence names the basic "inalienable rights" of every human being; the Bill of Rights acknowledges that the government has no legal power over those rights.

The rights in the First Amendment are examples of rights directly to *"life, liberty and the pursuit of happiness."* Religion, speech, press, and assembly are liberty rights that are necessary to pursue happiness. A person would be extraordinarily unhappy if the government was dictating what they could believe or say or with whom they could associate.

There is a direct correlation between the ideals of the Declaration of Independence and the rights in the Bill of Rights. The Bill of Rights carefully does not say the government "gives" anyone these rights, but rather it says that government cannot interfere with the "inalienable rights" that belong to everyone.

The Declaration of Independence lists the colonial complaints against the English king—is the Bill of Rights related to these complaints?

The Declaration of Independence lists twenty-eight complaints against King George. The complaints start with George's refusal to approve laws passed by colonial legislatures. The final complaint is that George has declined to even listen to any of the colonial grievances let alone do something about them. The entire list portrays George as a tyrant destroying the freedom of a people. The memory of this tyranny fueled demands for the Bill of Rights.

Provisions in the Bill of Rights address each complaint against the king. The Bill of Rights was designed to prevent the new American government from engaging in the same tyrannical conduct that lead to the Revolution. Beyond listing people's rights the first ten amendments are focused on limiting state tyranny by targeting the complaints outlined in the Declaration of Independence and taking precautions to protect the American people from such conduct by their own government.

The Bill of Rights, Volume Three

James Madison is sometimes referred to as the Father of the Constitution. While he was influential in the Constitutional Convention and a major contributor to the Federalist Papers, it is most accurate to refer to Madison as the Father of the Bill of Rights. Madison drafted nineteen proposed amendments, twelve were submitted to the states for ratification and ten were ratified, becoming the Bill of Rights.

Why was a Bill of Rights added to the United States Constitution?
After the Constitutional Convention finished its work on September 17, 1787, the proposed Constitution was sent to the states for ratification as provided for in Article VII. Ratification was by no means guaranteed. There were groups known as Federalists that favored ratification and the Anti-Federalists who opposed the Constitution.

The Anti-Federalists argued that the Constitution lacked specific protections for citizens from interference with their most important natural rights. The proposed Constitution did not protect citizens from the new government abusing citizens as the British had done. To secure votes for ratification over the objections to a lack of strong protections for citizen rights, proponents of the Constitution promised to amend the document by adding a Bill of Rights once the document was ratified. James Madison and the First Congress kept the promise by sending to the states amendments with protections against citizen abuse by the Federal government.

Did the Bill of Rights protect citizens from abuse of rights by state governments?

The Bill of Rights originally applied only to the federal government. The First Amendment demonstrates this clearly with the opening: *"Congress shall make no law . . ."* The state constitutions had their own bills of rights, and if citizens were to have protections from abuse by state governments they needed to look to their own courts and constitutions.

The 1776 Virginia Declaration of Rights drafted by George Mason served as a model for many states and the federal bill of rights. In 1868 the Fourteenth Amendment required the states to be governed by much of the federal Bill of Rights. The Fourteenth Amendment clearly restricts actions by state governments. It begins: *"No state shall make or enforce any law . . ."*

The Fourteenth Amendment requires states to follow *"due process of law"* and the federal Bill of Rights is considered a crucial element of the "due process" necessary to protect our liberties from every level of government.

Does the Bill of Rights protect its listed rights from infringement by all levels of government?

The First Amendment originally applied only to the federal government. With the Fourteenth Amendment in 1868, the Bill of Rights, including the First Amendment, restricted actions by state governments as well. The Fourteenth Amendment directs that no state shall deprive a person of either "due process" or "equal protection" of the law.

Over time these Fourteenth Amendment provisions have been interpreted to apply most of the Bill of Rights directly to state government actions. Examples of this are the First Amendment provisions regarding religion. In 1940 the Supreme Court applied the Free Exercise Clause to the states and in 1947 it applied the Establishment Clause.

Local governments, for example, cities, counties, townships and school boards, are created by state law. Once the Bill of Rights became a restriction on actions by the state government, it automatically became a restriction on actions by local governments as well.

Why are there ten amendments in the Bill of Rights?

James Madison's proposals for the Bill of Rights in the First Congress were a response to the Constitution's opponents, the Anti-Federalists who argued against the Constitution because it lacked protections for basic human liberty. Madison proposed nineteen amendments to the Congress. Twelve were approved by the Congress and sent to the states for ratification.

Of the twelve only ten articles were quickly ratified and became the First through Tenth Amendments. One of the two not approved, dealing with the number and apportionment of US Representatives, has never been approved. The other Article, limiting the ability of Congress to increase its members pay, became the Twenty-Seventh Amendment two hundred years later.

Though the two articles were proposed as part of the original "Bill of Rights," neither article included a right of the people or of the states. Despite the fact that there were twelve original proposals, the term "Bill of Rights" has come to mean only the ten amendments ratified in 1791.

The First Amendment

Congress shall make no law respecting
an establishment of religion, or prohibiting
the free exercise thereof; or abridging the
freedom of speech, or of the press; or the right
of the people peaceably to assemble, and to petition
the Government for a redress of grievances.

The First Amendment

Congress shall make no law respecting an establishment of re-ligion, or prohibiting the free exercise thereof; or abridging the freedom of speech, or of the press; or the right of the people peace-ably to assemble, and to petition the Government for a redress of grievances.

How many rights are named in the First Amendment and what are they?

Remembering this will place you among the one in one thousand Americans who can first state there are five rights involved in the First Amendment and second name the following:

- Freedom of Religion
- Freedom of Speech
- Freedom of the Press
- Freedom of Assembly
- Freedom to Petition for Redress of Grievances

The tone for the Bill of Rights is set with the opening of the First Amendment: *"Congress shall pass no law . . ."* Take a moment to reflect on that. The government may not pass a law.

The First Amendment's limits on government action in those five areas provide Americans with the most liberal Freedom of Expression anywhere in the world. These freedoms are not granted by the Constitution, they are simply acknowledged. The rights belong to ev-eryone as a matter of Natural Law as recognized by the Declaration of Independence with the phrase: *"the Law of Nature and of Nature's God."*

What is the first right addressed in the First Amendment?
Religious liberty is the first right mentioned in the First Amendment. The Constitution makes statements with its structure as well as with its words. The Congress is defined in Article I because the Founders considered it first among equals. The importance of religious liberty is demonstrated by its position as the first right of the First Amendment.

The First Amendment has two religious liberty clauses, The Establishment Clause and the Free Exercise Clause. The Establishment Clause prohibits government endorsement of a specific religion. The Free Exercise Clause prohibits government interference with the practice of religion.

This makes the United States different from many nations around the globe. England has an official religion (Anglican). Other countries are founded upon a specific religion (Muslim theocracy). Many communist countries such as China and Cuba, severely restrict the practice of religion in any form.

How is it fitting that religious liberty is the First Freedom?
The First Freedom acknowledged in the First Amendment is the Freedom of Religion. Seventeenth century European religious persecution arose from the belief, held by Protestants and Catholics, that a society must have religious uniformity since there was only a single true religion. Civil authorities had a duty to impose the single true religion by force if necessary in the interest of saving citizens' souls. Heretics might be executed and nonconformists were granted no mercy.

Religious persecution drove people from Europe to North America. In the seventeenth century, the English monarch headed the government's Church of England. Many disagreed with royal religious policies, and suffered physical punishment, imprisonment and loss of property as a result of holding firm to their religious convictions.

It is fitting that protection of religious liberty from government interference is America's "first freedom." Many of the first North American colonists were motivated by a search for religious liberty.

What is the "establishment" of religion?

The Establishment Clause forbids the federal government from proclaiming and financially supporting a national religion. A recognized national religion was common in many other countries at the time of the nation's founding. The First Amendment restricted the FEDERAL government's involvement in religion. When the Constitution was adopted all thirteen states provided government support in some way for religion. Support varied from tax benefits to religious requirements for voting or serving in the legislature. Eight states had "official religions."

It is less clear whether the Establishment Clause also prevents the federal government from supporting Christianity in general. The First Congress that proposed the Bill of Rights began the tradition of opening its sessions with prayer. That First Congress also voted to use federal dollars to establish Christian missions in the Indian lands. The writings by Thomas Jefferson and James Madison suggest the need to establish "a wall of separation" between church and state placing a far broader meaning on the Establishment Clause than was exhibited by the conduct of the First Congress.

What is the "free exercise" of religion?

The term "religious liberty" embraces the overall First Amendment religion concepts. Religious liberty is more than simply being able to go to the church of your choice. It is the right to live your life in a way consistent with your moral code without government interference.

That is the essence of "free exercise" of religion. As a result, everyone can choose a religion or form of worship without restrictions according to their conscience. "Free exercise" means that unless there is an important reason, the government cannot force people to violate their religious convictions. That is why, for example, there are exemptions from military service for conscientious objectors or why some traditional Native American churches may employ Peyote as a sacrament.

Just giving the name, religion, to a particular practice will not automatically provide exemptions to any law, but if a person has a strongly held belief, thanks to the Free Exercise Clause, the government needs to have an important reason to require violation of that belief.

Did the idea of religious tolerance start with those who came to North America to avoid persecution?

The Pilgrims are among the most well-known of those fleeing English religious persecution. They fled first to Holland in 1608. The Pilgrims left Holland because there was too much religious liberty. They feared their children would be corrupted by the Netherlands' religious tolerance.

In 1620 they set out for North America where their own "one true religion" could be practiced. Once established in their own colony, the Pilgrims enforced their own religious beliefs and banished non-conformists from their community.

Although the Pilgrims and other sects left England (and other European countries) to escape religious persecution, the belief of a governmental duty to impose religious purity traveled with them. By 1702, all thirteen colonies provided some form of state support for religion. Evolution toward the First Amendment's religious liberty was slow. Escaping from intolerance did not automatically give rise to tolerance.

Was there a long history of religious freedom in the states when the Constitution was written?

Commitment to freedom and self-government grew among the leaders of the New World, but government involvement in religion remained the rule rather than the exception. In 1779, three years after writing the Declaration of Independence, Thomas Jefferson, as Governor of Virginia, drafted the Virginia Act for Establishing Religious Freedom to end the use of tax money to support religion in Virginia. It did not become law while Jefferson was governor.

In 1784, Virginia Governor Patrick ("Give Me Liberty or Give Me Death") Henry introduced a bill calling for state support for "teachers of the Christian religion." Henry's bill was in keeping with traditional government support of religion and contrary to Jefferson's 1779 proposal. One hundred twenty four years after the Pilgrims arrived to establish their own religious liberty direct government involvement in religion remained part of the American landscape.

The Constitution was written in 1787 and the religious liberty clauses were added in 1791. These clauses were not applied to state governments officially until 1940. The evolution toward religious liberty throughout the United States was a more than 300 year process.

Is government "support" of religion actually a danger to religion?
The road to religious liberty was a winding one. In 1784 Virginia Governor Patrick Henry proposed a tax to support Christian teachers. James Madison's response provided the foundation for early American separation of church and state and for the First Amendment's religious liberty guarantees.

Madison opposed Henry's tax. Madison's successful opposition called attention to man's natural right in religious beliefs:

> *... the Religion then of every man must be left to the conviction and conscience of every ... man to exercise it as these may dictate. This right is in its nature an inalienable right.*

And the danger to religion of government involvement:

> *... that the same authority which can establish Christianity, in exclusion of all other Religions, may establish with the same ease any particular sect of Christians, in exclusion of all other Sects?*

Due to Madison's arguments, Henry's proposed law for a tax to support Christian instruction was defeated. It also created the atmosphere for the religious liberty guarantees of the First Amendment seven years later.

Does the First Amendment require a "wall of separation" between the church and state?
In 1791, First Amendment protections of religious liberty from the new federal government became the law of the land with two clauses, the "Establishment Clause" and the "Free Exercise Clause":

> *Congress shall make no law respecting an establishment of religion, or prohibiting the free exercise thereof...*

The idea of a wall between the church and state is not found in the First Amendment. The "wall of separation" phrase arose in a letter Thomas Jefferson wrote as president in 1802, eleven years after the First Amendment was ratified:

> *I contemplate with sovereign reverence that act of the whole American people which declared that their legislature should "make no law respecting an establishment of religion or prohibiting the free exercise thereof," thus building a wall of separation between church and State.*

Does the Free Speech Clause protect just speech?

The First Amendment's Free Speech Clause prohibits Congress from limiting the manner in which individuals express themselves. This not only applies to written and spoken words, but also to symbolic expressions such as art and music. Free speech includes demonstrative expressions of ideas such as symbolic armbands to protest a war or burning the US flag as a form of political protest.

Freedom of speech has limitations. The government cannot limit speech involving political thoughts and ideas, but the First Amendment does not constitutionally protect all speech.

The best example of unprotected speech is falsely yelling "fire" in a crowded theater. The government can also punish false speech defined as defamation or libel. Generally, the government may not restrict speech that is either truthful or expresses an opinion.

What is the role of Natural Law in the recognition of the right to Free Speech?

The American concept of free speech grew from a union of Natural Law, individual sovereignty, the need for free and open discussion in Congress and the right to serve in Congress. When it was added, the First Amendment's Free Speech command: *"Congress shall make no law . . . abridging the freedom of speech . . ."* was unlike any restriction on government in the history of mankind.

Through history the right to criticize government had been restricted to the upper echelons of society. Roman senators and English members of Parliament could speak freely. Nearly everyone else could not. In the new American republic, this would not be the case, there would be free speech for everyone.

The Declaration of Independence's references to the Laws of Nature and Nature's God demonstrate the importance of Natural Law theory in the origins of the United States.

Individual sovereignty is a component of Natural Law. This sovereignty is the underpinning of the legitimacy of the United States, and ultimately the right to free speech. At America's founding the idea of free speech for the general population was a radical idea.

Does Freedom of the Press apply only to newspapers?
When the Bill of Rights was ratified, the press was newspaper and books. This was the case for nearly 100 years until electronic communications became accessible to the general population. The idea of Freedom of the Press adapted as communications methods evolved demonstrating the application and relevance of 200-year-old constitutional principles to a changing world.

Freedom of the Press covers radio, television and the internet. This has not been without a struggle. Concepts like the "Fairness Doctrine" remain in debate about government regulation of television and radio. Proposals in Congress about internet regulation bring technological innovation into conflict with Free Speech principles.

The First Amendment's Free Press Clause has given rise to important concepts including a reporter's privilege to protect his sources, and limits on government regulating information prior to its publication, banning "prior restraint."

How was the development of American "Free Press" revolutionary in human history?
The exceptional American concept that a free press was a necessary element of representative government did not come from English tradition. There was a long history of licensing of the press in England by kings and then by Parliament. Before America it was necessary to have the permission of the government to publish a newspaper.

Besides licensing laws that gave the English government control over who could operate a printing press, there was also the common law crime of seditious libel. Seditious libel was a printed statement that "brings into hatred or contempt" the monarch or his family or the government. The possible penalty for printing such material was life in prison.

The English controls on the press were inconsistent with the developing American freedoms. The idea that private parties could publish information without government interference was truly revolutionary.

How did the Right to Petition for Redress of Grievances develop in colonial America?

The Right to Petition was central to constitutional law and politics in the early United States. It is the First Amendment's capstone, yet The Right to Petition is unknown to most Americans. If known, it's thought of as extension of the first four rights, and not a right standing on its own. This is because its history is unknown as well.

In the American Colonies petitioning became the act of submitting grievances to local legislative assemblies. By the early eighteenth century, Americans submitted a wide range of petitions to the locally elected houses of assembly. The right to petition included the right to consideration. Colonial petitions addressed a wide range of subjects including religion and the established church, slavery, debt (public and private), taxes, divorce, appeals from judicial decisions, naturalization and more.

Petitions were submitted by men, women, children and slaves. The elected bodies of the colonies understood their duty was to entertain the petitions of all. This was the background of petitioning when the Declaration of Independence was drafted.

Had the colonies asked King George to "redress" their grievances before declaring independence?

The Continental Congress had sent multiple messages to King George with their complaints about the deprivation of rights and freedoms. The King's response to colonial grievances was among the complaints listed in the Declaration of Independence:

In every stage of these Oppressions We have Petitioned for Redress in the most humble terms: Our repeated Petitions have been answered only by repeated injury. A Prince whose character is thus marked by every act which may define a Tyrant, is unfit to be the ruler of a free people.

This experience resulted in including the freedom to petition the government for redress of grievances in the First Amendment. Largely ignored, Americans have allowed this guarantee to become nonfunctioning, something that should not happen to any word of the Constitution.

What has changed in the Right to Petition for Redress of Grievances?

As a warning to what happens when people do not study or exercise their rights, the Right to Petition with the implied right that the petition be seriously considered has disappeared. People can write letters to their representatives and communicate in other ways, but the obligation of the government to actually respond as existed when the First Amendment was adopted is no longer recognized.

This started shortly before the Civil War when Congress was inundated with petitions to abolish slavery. Until the years before the Civil War, Congress routinely entertained citizen Petitions pursuant to the Petition Clause. The growth of petitions regarding slavery were an embarrassment to southern states and the House of Representatives adopted the Gag Rule, prohibiting petitions to abolish slavery.

Though the Gag Rule was later rescinded Congress's approach to petitions was changed. It has never recovered and despite the provision in the First Amendment the people no longer have the right to have their representatives entertain their petitions.

A right not exercised will be lost. The fate of the "Right to Petition for Redress of Grievances" should be a warning that all rights must be defended.

A well regulated Militia, being necessary to the security of a free State, the right of the people to keep and bear Arms, shall not be infringed

SECOND AMENDMENT

The Second Amendment:
The Right to Bear Arms

A well regulated Militia, being necessary to the security of a free State, the right of the people to keep and bear Arms, shall not be infringed.

What is meant by a "well-regulated militia"?

A militia consisted of male citizens who could be brought together for protecting the community from threats. These threats could be from outside forces, bandits or in those days, Indians. Many local laws required citizens to own a gun and to be available to meet communal threats. It was local militias at Lexington and Concord Massachusetts that engaged the British army in the first armed conflict of the Revolution.

The militia was the local "army" of citizens who looked after the security of the community.

The Second Amendment's militia provision protected the right of the people to maintain a well-regulated militia. Like many Bill of Rights provisions it responded to concerns raised during the ratification debates. The particular concern was that Congress might attempt to deactivate state militias and replace them with a national standing army.

The memory of the need to respond with arms to a tyrannical far away government was fresh in many minds.

Does the right to bear arms belong to an individual or is it connected with "militia" service?

There have been two principle interpretations of the Second Amendment. One view is that it protects the rights of individuals to own weapons with limited government restrictions. The other theory is that the Second Amendment means that possession of arms shall be protected for the collective defense of the community and that strict regulation of private ownership is constitutional.

The phrase *"well-regulated militia"* is relied upon by supporters of strict gun control laws to mean that constitutionally protected gun ownership is limited to militias as they were understood in the late eighteenth century.

The world as it existed in 1791 was much different than today. There were not well organized law enforcement agencies. Self-defense and personal protection were the norm. Many people relied upon hunting for feeding their families. Personal gun ownership was a practical necessity. This history leads many people to believe the meaning of *"the right of the people to keep and bear Arms, shall not be infringed"* indicates a right to personal gun ownership.

This debate raged for many years between advocates of strong gun control and those favoring limited regulation.

Why is there a right to bear arms?

Since 1791, until recent times, the Supreme Court had little to say about the Second Amendment. There was only one significant case: *United States v. Miller*, decided in 1939. Then in 2008, *District of Columbia v. Heller* was decided and put the debate to rest.

> *There seems to us no doubt, on the basis of both text and history, that the Second Amendment conferred an individual right to keep and bear arms.*
>
> —Justice Antonin Scalia

The Supreme Court resolved the debate in *Heller* in favor of a personal natural right. The Court's resolution traced the individual right to bear arms to the natural right of self-defense.

The first inalienable natural right is to life. The logical extension of the right to life is the right to self-defense. At the time of America's founding, Sir William Blackstone was well known in the American colonies. He described the most important of rights as: "the natural right of resistance and self-preservation," and "the right of having and using arms for self-preservation and defence . . ."

Ultimately: "*The right to self-defence is the first law of nature . . .*"

The Third Amendment: No Quartering of Soldiers

No soldier shall, in time of peace, be quartered in any house without the consent of the owner, nor in time of war, but in a manner to be prescribed by law.

The Constitution's Third Amendment has never been the controlling law in any case decided by the US Supreme Court, and has been of critical importance in only one appellate case in the nation's history. It is often ignored and in some ways considered nonfunctioning having been a response to an archaic military practice. It has found life in the twenty-first century in other ways, because the same as every other provision in the Constitution it decides a question between power and liberty.

Why did the Founders feel the need for a constitutional prohibition on government soldiers in people's homes?

The Third Amendment, like many other provisions of the Bill of Rights responded to colonial grievances against King George. The Declaration of Independence listed twenty-eight complaints against the King, among them: "*... quartering large bodies of armed troops among us...*" In 1765 and 1774 Parliament passed laws requiring American colonists to shelter and feed British soldiers. The Quartering Act of 1774 was among the Intolerable Acts that set the table for the American Revolution.

In 1765, Parliament ordered that British soldiers in the colonies be housed in barracks, public houses, private commercial property, and uninhabited homes. The Quartering Act of 1774 added to the 1765 act requiring colonists to house troops in private homes as well.

Property owners received no compensation and, in fact, were mandated to provide soldiers with necessities such as food, liquor, salt, and bedding, also without compensation. It was crucial that the new government would not do this to American citizens.

What famous saying is at the root of the Third Amendment?
The Third Amendment stands for a proposition that had been fundamental to free Englishmen at least since the sixteenth century and best expressed by Sir Edward Coke in 1628: "For a man's house is his castle, et *domus sua cuique*."

Coke expressed an English principle that had been ignored by the British in the colonies. Fresh in the memories of the Founding generation, the response was the Third Amendment.

The colonial objection to having soldiers in their homes was not forgotten when the Revolution ended and the Constitution was proposed. During the ratification debates in 1788–89 there was concern that the proposed Constitution did not contain specific protections for citizens from government abuse. The Third Amendment can be traced to the phrase: "*A man's home is his castle*" and the abuse of this principle by the British.

When were the greatest violations of the Third Amendment?
During congressional debates about the first constitutional amendments in 1789, South Carolina Rep. Thomas Sumter's thoughts were recorded in the official proceedings as follows: "*Mr. Sumter hoped soldiers would never be quartered on the inhabitants, either in time of peace or war, without the consent of the owner*," because otherwise "*their property would lie at the mercy of men irritated by a refusal, and well-disposed to destroy the peace of the family*."

Third Amendment violations happened during the American Civil War. Forced quartering of Union soldiers occurred "*in a manner*" which was not "*prescribed by law*" and without the "*consent of the owner*." A congressional declaration of war never was passed against the Confederate States and Congress never passed a law authorizing the quartering. This means that the forced quartering in loyal Union states violated both Third Amendment provisions.

The April 12, 1861 attack on Fort Sumter launched the Civil War. During the War, despite the Third Amendment, the 1789 warnings of Congressman Sumter, for whom the fort was named, came to pass.

Has the Supreme Court relied upon the Third Amendment to uphold other rights?

The Supreme Court has viewed the Third Amendment's personal privacy philosophy as giving expression to the Constitution's establishment of a limited government and the Ninth Amendment's non-enumerated rights. The Third Amendment denotes what is public and what is private and expresses the crucial sense of privacy of America's Founders.

The Third Amendment was among the founding provisions used to define the right to privacy in *Griswold v. Connecticut*. The 1965 case overturned a Connecticut law restricting distribution and use of contraceptives and pointed to the Third Amendment as building into the Constitution a Right of Privacy.

Supreme Court Justice Story best states the Third Amendment's value in his *Commentaries on the Constitution*: "*This provision speaks for itself. Its plain object is to secure the perfect enjoyment of that great right of the common law, that a man's house shall be his own castle, privileged against all civil and military intrusion . . .*" The Third Amendment expressed revulsion at a British military practice and resulted in a principle, that of a right to domestic privacy, relevant in the twenty-first century.

Are there more twenty-first century applications of the Third Amendment?

At the time the Third Amendment was ratified, the images and memories of British troops in shops and homes in Boston and other cities were still fresh, and the clashes with colonists that drew the country into war still evoked strong emotions.

What did not exist at the time was a uniformed and armed "police force." That development was far in the future. However, the Third

Amendment expresses a philosophy used to define a "right to privacy" from the government. It means that armed men of the government are prohibited from commandeering a home. As the modern police force has become more "militarized" there is a belief that the Third Amendment applies to that element of government though the "police" are not soldiers in the traditional sense.

The Third Amendment is not a stunted appendage of the Constitution. The Third Amendment did decide a question between power and liberty. It is perilous to freedom to think of any portion of the document as nonfunctioning.

The 4th Amendment

The right of the people to be secure in their persons, houses, papers, and effects, against unreasonable searches and seizures, shall not be violated, and no warrants shall issue, but upon probable cause, supported by oath or affirmation, and particularly describing the place to be searched, and the persons or things to be seized.

The Fourth Amendment

The right of the people to be secure in their persons, houses, papers, and effects, against unreasonable searches and seizures, shall not be violated, and no warrants shall issue, but upon probable cause, supported by oath or affirmation, and particularly describing the place to be searched, and the persons or things to be seized.

What was a "Writ of Assistance" and how did it lead to the Fourth Amendment?

A "writ of assistance" was a particular type of "general warrant" used by the British to search colonial property before the Revolution. The Fourth Amendment responded to King George's "general warrants" which did not respect the sanctity of private property. The Fourth Amendment, like the Third Amendment, is rooted in the English tradition of the sanctity of one's home.

The king's "general warrants" did not define a place to be searched or items sought. A general warrant lasted for the king's lifetime plus six months. A king's agent with a general warrant had almost unrestricted power to search anywhere.

In 1760 properties belonging to Boston merchants were the main targets of "writs of assistance" searches. They resisted the writs in colonial courtrooms and lost. The cases set in motion events that lead not just to the Fourth Amendment, but to the American Revolution.

The lessons learned from Britain's misuse of general warrants resulted in a ban on "general warrants" by requiring probable cause and details of the location to be searched and person or items to be seized.

What inalienable right from the Declaration of Independence does the Fourth Amendment protect?

The Fourth Amendment protects the inalienable right to liberty noted in the Declaration of Independence. Any detention or interference with a citizen's liberty by a law enforcement official, however brief, is a seizure for Fourth Amendment purposes.

A person is under arrest or seized when the police detain someone in such a way that it is clear he is not free to leave. A person can be "under arrest" without an announcement by the police and without handcuffs or physical restraint.

A person is arrested or seized when by any show of authority his liberty is restrained. A traffic stop is an arrest. When a reasonable person does not feel free to leave an encounter with law enforcement an arrest has taken place. In those circumstances for the citizen's detention to be legal there must either be a warrant or probable cause. This requirement is a protection for our liberty.

What is a warrant and how do the police get one?

A warrant is a document issued by a judge authorizing the police or some other body to make an arrest, search places or premises relating to the administration of justice.

Unless a specific exception applies the Fourth Amendment requires that searches, seizures, and arrests be conducted pursuant to a lawfully executed warrant.

A request for a warrant must contain a sworn, detailed statement made by a law enforcement officer appearing before a neutral judge or magistrate. The detailed statement explains to the judge why probable cause exists to conduct the search or arrest. The requesting officer must swear that the facts in the request are to the best of his knowledge.

The Fourth Amendment also requires that a warrant "particularly" describe the person or place to be searched or seized. Warrants must provide enough detail so that an officer with the warrant can identify the persons and places identified in the warrant.

Can a police officer make an arrest or conduct a search without a warrant?

When the Fourth Amendment was adopted warrantless arrests were allowed in public when there was a breach of the peace or a felony had been committed. These types of arrests or seizures of the person continue to be allowed under the Fourth Amendment with probable cause.

Probable cause is the legal standard by which a police officer has the authority to make an arrest, conduct a personal or property search, or obtain a warrant for arrest. While many factors contribute to a police officer's level of authority in a given situation, probable cause requires facts or evidence that would lead a reasonable person to believe that a suspect has committed a crime. The test to determine whether probable cause exists for a legal arrest is whether the officer's knowledge of facts and circumstances are sufficient to lead a prudent person to believe a suspect has committed, is committing, or is about to commit a crime.

This test indicates that mere suspicion of a crime is not enough, but the standard for probable cause is a reasonable suspicion of criminality and not actual or certain knowledge.

If an officer makes an arrest without a warrant must he still answer to a judge?

Even though an arrest may be made without a warrant based upon probable cause, such an arrest must be justified to a judge within a reasonable time. The Supreme Court addressed this issue in *Gerstein v.*

Pugh. A person detained without a warrant must be brought before a judge to determine if the officer had probable cause to make the arrest.

Evidence is given to the judge relating to "probable cause." The Fourth Amendment requires a judicial determination of probable cause even post arrest.

The issues of *Gerstein* are only two:

- Is there some evidence a crime was committed?
- Is there some evidence that this individual was involved?

What are the consequences in a criminal prosecution if a police officer conducts a search or arrest without a warrant?

The Fourth Amendment announces the right to be free from unreasonable searches and seizures, but the manner of enforcing that right is not specified. If a criminal prosecution results from a Fourth Amendment violation by the government, evidence obtained as a result of a violation may not be presented at a trial. The evidence is excluded from trial, hence the Exclusionary Rule.

There are three elements to the Exclusionary Rule. These elements are:

- The seizure of property without a warrant by a police officer, or by someone acting as an agent of the police.
- There must be evidence for use in a criminal prosecution obtained or seized.
- There must be a connection between the illegal action and the evidence obtained. If there is an illegal action, but the action was unrelated to the collection of evidence, the state may present the evidence at trial.

Are the police always required to obtain a warrant to conduct a search?

The Fourth Amendment search warrant requirement has six major exceptions.

1. Search Incident to Lawful Arrest
A search incident to lawful arrest does not require issuance of a warrant. If someone is lawfully arrested, the police may legally search his person.

2. Plain View Exception
Police may seize evidence in plain view if they are legally in the area from which the evidence can be viewed.

3. Consent
If consent is given by a person reasonably believed by an officer to have authority to give such consent, no warrant is required for a search or seizure.

4. Stop & Frisk
Police may stop a suspect if there is a reasonable suspicion of a criminal act.

5. Automobile Exception
A warrant is not required to search vehicles if police have probable cause to believe the vehicle contains evidence of a crime.

6. Emergencies/Hot Pursuit
Evidence that can be easily moved or destroyed before a warrant can be issued may be seized without a warrant.

Are there other remedies for violations of the Fourth Amendment?

There are at least two alternatives as ways to deter illegal conduct by police officers. One is to charge police with crimes for illegally entering homes and buildings or someone's property. As a practical matter, police are members of law enforcement and criminal or even administrative sanctions against police are rare.

There is the possibility of privately enforcing Fourth Amendment rights through a civil suit seeking money from the police officers that committed the violation and the agency he works for.

An individual who has had his property or person illegally searched or seized may sue the police for money damages. Since most cases of police misconduct are decided by juries from the community who have been taught to respect and honor law enforcement jury awards are likely in only the most serious Fourth Amendment violations.

This may be changing with modern technology recording more video of police/citizen encounters, a favorable development for the Fourth Amendment.

The Fifth Amendment: The Right to Remain Silent and Four More

No person shall be held to answer for a capital, or otherwise infamous crime, unless on a presentment or indictment of a grand jury, except in cases arising in the land or naval forces, or in the militia, when in actual service in time of war or public danger; nor shall any person be subject for the same offense to be twice put in jeopardy of life or limb; nor shall be compelled in any criminal case to be a witness against himself, nor be deprived of life, liberty, or property, without due process of law; nor shall private property be taken for public use, without just compensation.

How many rights are in the Fifth Amendment and what are they?
The Fifth Amendment contains five rights. These rights are "procedural" rights. People are entitled to the benefits of these constitutional procedures as protections for their inalienable rights.

The Fifth Amendment's first four rights define procedures involving grand juries, double jeopardy, self-incrimination, and due process. These procedures are to protect a person's life and liberty from government action. The fifth procedure is designed to protect property, preventing the government from taking property without compensation to the owner.

The Fifth Amendment's protections for life, liberty and property exist to limit the government's interference with the inalienable natural rights of the Declaration of Independence. John Locke, the philosophical father of the Declaration, defined the right to benefit from one's labor, that is to own property, as the third inalienable right. Thomas Jefferson substituted "pursuit of happiness" for "property" in writing the Declaration.

How are grand juries intended to protect freedom?

Grand juries appeared in English law with the Magna Carta in 1215. The idea was to place citizens between those accused of a crime and prosecution by the King. Grand jury protections were seen as a citizen's shield from improper government prosecutions.

Prior to the American Revolution, as tensions grew between the colonies and England, colonial grand juries regularly refused to approve the king's prosecutions. The power of colonial grand juries was used to lead the revolution to oppose British rule and exercise the rights of self-government.

The Fifth Amendment requires that before the federal government can prosecute someone for a felony (*capital, or otherwise infamous crime*) it must present the evidence to a grand jury. A prosecutor presents evidence to a group of citizens (grand jurors) and those citizens determine, by a majority, if the government has enough evidence to indict (accuse) and prosecute someone for a crime.

What is the protection against "double jeopardy"?

The Double Jeopardy Clause, *nor shall any person be subject for the same offense to be twice put in jeopardy of life or limb*, protects an individual from successive prosecutions for the same alleged act, to ensure the integrity of a not guilty finding, and to protect a defendant from the emotional, psychological, physical, and financial difficulties attached to multiple trials for the same alleged offense. The Double Jeopardy Clause includes three different rights. The right:

- To not face a second prosecution following a not guilty verdict
- To not face a second prosecution following a guilty verdict
- To not receive multiple punishments for the same offense

For the Clause to apply the first question is if "jeopardy" has "attached." A defendant becomes in danger of a guilty finding once a trial begins and at that point "jeopardy" has "attached" and the protections of the clause kick in. Double Jeopardy protections apply to both federal and state prosecutions.

What does it mean to "plead the Fifth"?
The best known Fifth Amendment protection is the right to remain silent. It applies not only to criminal defendants, but others from being forced to give testimony or make statements that may be used against them in a criminal prosecution. A witness in a proceeding, other than the defendant, may "plead the Fifth" and decline to answer questions if the witness reasonably believes such answers may implicate him in criminal activity.

The *Miranda* warnings advise criminal suspects of their right to remain silent. Advice to a suspect of his right to counsel comes from the Sixth Amendment. When law enforcement takes a suspect into custody, a suspect must be made aware of his rights. If law enforcement fails to inform a suspect of his rights, any evidence obtained may not be used against the defendant in a trial. This is similar to the exclusionary rule applied to Fourth Amendment violations. These Fifth and Sixth Amendment guarantees apply equally to state and federal governments.

What are the *Miranda* Warnings and what happened to Miranda?
The *Miranda* warnings are part of American criminal justice and American popular culture.

Ernesto Miranda was the name of a twenty-three-year-old Mexican immigrant. In his 1966 case, *Miranda v. Arizona*, the United States Supreme Court in 1966 required that police must advise a suspect of several constitutional rights prior to interrogation. If the police do not, any statements made by the suspect may not be used against him in prosecuting a crime.

The warnings became known as "Miranda Warnings." Ernesto Miranda's name has even become a verb: to Mirandize. The standard warnings are:

> *You have the right to remain silent. Anything you say can and will be used against you in a court of law. You have the right to have an attorney present during questioning. If you cannot afford an attorney, one will be appointed for you.*

A footnote to the story: In 1976 Miranda was killed in a Phoenix bar. A suspect was arrested in his killing. The suspect was advised of his right to remain silent and did so. No one was ever convicted in the killing of Ernesto Miranda. (Miranda's picture is at the beginning of this chapter.)

What is the guarantee of Due Process?

This clause enshrines the "rule of law" into the Constitution. It can be traced to a phrase in the 1215 *Magna Carta*. That phrase, "law of the land" would, over the centuries, become "due process of law." The idea that a person should not have his property or liberty taken by the government except by pre-existing law and procedures has become known as the "rule of law." This means there must be established procedures and laws in place before someone suffers a loss at the hands of the government. Additionally those laws and procedures are to be administered by an impartial third party.

Due process is guaranteed for all citizens regarding the rights, guarantees, and protections provided by the US Constitution and all laws passed under the Constitution's authority. Absent due process the government cannot deprive someone of life, liberty, or property.

Due process guarantees a judicial proceeding that is fundamentally fair, orderly, impartial and just. The Fifth Amendment Due Process Clause applies only to the federal government. Rights to Due Process in state proceedings were guaranteed by identical language in the Fourteenth Amendment.

What is Just Compensation for when a government takes private property?

The concept of eminent domain permits the government to take private property for public use. The Just Compensation Clause requires a government, whether local, state or federal, to compensate the property owner whose property is taken.

Just compensation has been interpreted as fair market value, defined by what a willing, unpressured buyer would pay in an arm's length transaction between unrelated parties. The process typically involves an offer by the government to purchase a property. If the government and owner do not agree on the value, a jury will decide.

Governments can also owe property owners compensation when they pass regulations or zoning laws that affect the value of the property.

Historically, "public use" was considered to be for roads, public utilities or buildings. In 2005, the concept of public use was controversially extended by the Supreme Court to include government taking property from a private owner to make that property available for private commercial development. Many states have responded to that decision by passing laws limiting their own eminent domain powers to taking property only for traditional public uses.

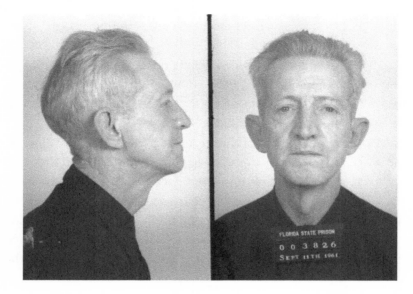

The Sixth Amendment: Right to Counsel and Five More

In all criminal prosecutions, the accused shall enjoy the right to a speedy and public trial, by an impartial jury of the state and district wherein the crime shall have been committed, which district shall have been previously ascertained by law, and to be informed of the nature and cause of the accusation; to be confronted with the witnesses against him; to have compulsory process for obtaining witnesses in his favor, and to have the assistance of counsel for his defense.

How many rights are in the Sixth Amendment and what are they?
The Sixth Amendment contains rights beyond the well-known right to an attorney in criminal matters. There are six constitutional rights in the Sixth Amendment. They are procedural rights designed to protect an individual's inalienable natural rights of life and liberty.

A summary of Sixth Amendment rights:

- Right to a speedy trial
- Right to a public trial
- Right to an impartial jury trial in the place where the crime was committed
- Right to be informed of the charges
- Right to confront the witnesses against him and to subpoena witnesses
- Right to an attorney

Originally these rights were only guaranteed to persons charged with federal crimes. The Due Process Clause of the Fourteenth Amendment has extended these rights to cover state criminal proceedings.

What is the right to a speedy trial?

The right to a speedy trial has been defined by statute in most jurisdictions, placing time limitations during which a criminal trial must take place, or else the charges must be dismissed.

There is a four part test to determine if speedy trial rights have been violated:

- Length of Delay: A delay of a year or more from the date on which the speedy trial right "attaches" (the date of arrest or indictment, whichever first occurs) was termed "presumptively prejudicial"
- Reason for the delay: The government may not delay a trial for its own benefit, but a trial may be delayed for the testimony of an absent witness or other practical reasons.
- Time and manner in which the defendant has asserted his right: If a defendant agrees to a delay or causes it himself when the delay is beneficial to the defendant, he cannot later claim violation of his speedy trial right.
- Degree of prejudice to the defendant by the delay.

Does a trial absolutely have to be held in public?

The public-trial right comes from the Founders' sense of history and knowledge of the secret proceedings held in England beginning with the Star Chamber in 1487, in which criminal charges were pressed outside of public view.

The public trial right is not absolute. The prosecution or defense may request a closed trial. The right to a public trial must be balanced against the right to a fair trial. If the court finds a public trial will interfere with the trial's fairness, the proceedings may be closed. These are rare circumstances.

The idea of a public trial is to protect the defendant's liberty by having the proceedings observed by anyone who wishes, thus promoting a fair trial. A defendant may choose to give up his right to a public trial, but he does not have an absolute right to a private trial. There is a First Amendment Freedom of the Press issue that prevents the government from sealing otherwise public proceedings. There may be times a defendant wishes a private trial, but the press has a right to view the proceedings.

What is the Right to a Jury in criminal cases?
In a criminal case, the government prosecutes or charges a defendant with a violation of the criminal law and begins proceedings (bail hearings, arraignments and trials) to prove that charge beyond a reasonable doubt.

The Sixth Amendment provides many protections and rights to a person accused of a crime. One right is to have his or her case heard by an impartial jury—independent people from the surrounding community who are willing to decide the case based only on the evidence. In some cases where there has been a significant amount of news coverage, the Supreme Court has ruled that jury members may be picked from another location in order to ensure that the jurors are impartial.

When choosing a jury, both prosecutors and defense attorneys may object to certain people being included. Some of these objections, called challenges, are for cause (the potential juror has said or done something that shows he or she may not act fairly). Others are peremptory (no real reason need be given, but one side does not want to have that person serve). Lawyers cannot use peremptory challenges to keep people off a jury because of race or gender.

Isn't the right to be informed of the charges against you a bit obvious?
It certainly seems obvious and fair that when the government charges someone with a crime that the person be told what law he has violated and what he did to violate that law. That a government does not always conduct itself in a fair manner and that it needs to be reminded of the obvious is found in this provision of the Sixth Amendment.

Dating at least back to the twelfth century, English court systems could proceed with charges like heresy on the mere suggestion of "ill fame" without the need for detail. Four hundred years later the High Commission and Star Chamber brought in citizens and questioned them without stating the nature of the allegation.

As colonists emigrated from Europe to America to escape religious persecution and tyrannical government they began adopting a requirement for informing an accused of the charges in detail. This requirement took root and became fundamental in America.

History had shown that a right so fair and obvious still needed protection from the proposed new government under the Constitution. James Madison's proposal for this clause was adopted without debate and placed in the Sixth Amendment.

Was the United States the first government to formally require informing a defendant of charges?

There have been many gifts to the world from America's Founding. This provision of the Sixth Amendment is among them. The right of an accused to be informed of the charges against him has found its way into multiple international agreements. An example is found in the international agreement that forms The Organization for Security and Co-operation in Europe (OSCE):

> *6.3.1 The right to be informed of criminal charges*
> *Article 14(3) (a) of the ICCPR and Article 6(3) (a) of the ECHR guarantee the right of every person accused of a "criminal charge" or "criminal offence" to be informed promptly, in detail, and in a language which the accused understands, of the nature (legal characterization of the offence) and cause (alleged facts) of the charge.*

Before America's Sixth Amendment, what seems so fair and obvious had never been the firm commitment of any government in the world. It is now the standard for the world. This is the type of idea that should be encompassed by the phrase "American Exceptionalism."

Why is there a constitutional right for a defendant to confront the witnesses against him?

Sir Walter Raleigh is known for many things. Raleigh's contribution to the US Constitution was his demand that he be able to face the witness against him during his trial for treason in 1603.

Raleigh's demand was denied and a written statement of an alleged co-conspirator was used as evidence against him, without the witness appearing in court to answer questions about the statement. Raleigh was convicted and spent the next thirteen years in prison.

In England and British North America during the seventeenth century courts did not require the personal appearance of witnesses in court. Prosecutors customarily used witness depositions instead of live courtroom testimony despite defendant demands for face-to-face confrontation. Injustices similar to that suffered by Raleigh took place during America's revolutionary era. America's Founders were well aware of Raleigh's famous case and their own colonial experiences were fresh in their minds. This knowledge and experience led to protections for the right of confrontation in the United States.

What does the Right of Confrontation mean?

The Sixth Amendment requires that if there is testimony at trial given by witnesses it cannot be done by a written statement, but rather must be done in person and the defendant must have the opportunity to ask the witness questions (confront the witness). This right only applies at a trial. The right does not apply to information supplied by an informant or other information supplied by persons who do not testify at trial. An additional right that is a logical extension of the right to confront witnesses is a defendant's right to be present at trial. This means that a trial cannot be held when the defendant is absent. The defendant may give up his right to be present should he so choose. If he does so the trial may proceed without him.

There have been many modern accommodations to the right of confrontation coming from technological advances that allow witnesses to testify and be cross-examined remotely, but the principle that there is a requirement for live testimony survives.

Did criminal defendants always have a right to appointed lawyers in American courts?

Thanks to television police reading the Miranda Warnings, people are familiar with a criminal defendant's right to an attorney and that an indigent defendant may have appointed counsel. Such protections have not always been part of United States law.

In England and early colonial America, criminal defendants were denied counsel on the theory that a guilty defendant should not escape punishment because of a skilled attorney. While the Sixth Amendment changed this practice, for 141 years the right to counsel was understood to *allow* a defendant to hire a lawyer for his defense. The state was not required to provide counsel for a poor defendant.

In 1932, with the case of the "Scottsboro Boys," an evolution began leading to a universal right to an attorney for anyone accused of a crime. Nine young black defendants in that case had been charged with rape, convicted and sentenced to death within two weeks of the alleged crime, without the benefit of competent counsel. For the first time, the Supreme Court held that because of the "special circumstances" of the case they were entitled to court appointed counsel that the defendants chose. The convictions and death sentences were overturned.

This was the case that began changing how the right to counsel was understood. Before *Gideon* a defendant had the right to *hire* a lawyer. After Gideon, a poor defendant has the right to an appointed lawyer paid for by the government.

Does the right to counsel now apply to all criminal defendants?

Thanks to the 1963 case of *Gideon v. Wainwright,* if a criminal defendant faces the possibility of six months or more in jail, he is entitled to a court appointed attorney, and without cost if he cannot afford one.

The story of that change started when Clarence Gideon was charged with having broken into and entered a poolroom. Gideon appeared in court indigent and without a lawyer. He asked the court to appoint counsel for him. His request was denied. Gideon was found guilty and sentenced to five years in prison.

From the Florida State Prison a pencil written appeal of Gideon's conviction was sent to the US Supreme Court. The handwritten appeal argued that Gideon had been denied his Sixth Amendment right to appointed counsel.

The Supreme Court overturned Gideon's conviction. In doing so, the Court said that the Sixth Amendment right to counsel applied to all state criminal prosecutions, and that the states were obligated to appoint counsel for indigent defendants. Gideon was given a new trial and a court appointed attorney. The jury found him not guilty in less than an hour. (Clarence Gideon's picture is at the beginning of this chapter.)

I consider trial by jury as the only anchor ever yet imagined by man, by which a government can be held to the principles of its constitution.

--Jefferson

The Seventh Amendment: Right to Jury in Federal Civil Cases

*In Suits at common law, where the value in controversy shall ex-
ceed twenty dollars, the right of trial by jury shall be preserved,
and no fact tried by a jury, shall be otherwise re-examined in any
Court of the United States, than according to the rules of the common law.*

How do juries fit into the scheme of constitutional government?
The Founding Fathers feared government power. They found citizen
juries to be a critical check on that power. King George's suspension
of jury trials was one of the Declaration of Independence grievances.
The Constitution's Seventh Amendment reflects colonial history and
beliefs.

John Adams described the place of the jury in the system of government:

> *... the Constitution ... requires that the common people, should
> have as complete a control, as decisive a negative, in every judg-
> ment of a court of judicature.*

Although the original Constitution contained a provision for jury
trials in criminal cases in Article III, Section 2, Clause 3, there was no
provision for jury trials in civil cases. During the ratification debates,
the Constitution's opponents pointed out this deficiency, and its proponents promised the First Congress would propose an amendment
to address this issue.

This reflected the Founders' skepticism of government and faith in the people to act as the protectors of each other's liberty.

What is the purpose of the Seventh Amendment?
The Seventh Amendment provides for juries to decide questions in civil lawsuits in federal court. Civil cases settle disputes between private parties and claims for money by citizens against the government or by the government against citizens. Money damages are the primary remedy in a civil suit. The Seventh Amendment guarantees a jury trial in Federal Court in civil cases. It does not apply to civil cases in state courts.

In adding this provision, the Founders affirmed the critical role of jurors in protecting a citizen's inalienable right to possess the fruits of his labor.

Article III of the Constitution required jury trials in criminal cases before there were any amendments. Opponents of the Constitution had complained that there was no requirement for juries in civil trials. The Seventh Amendment was added to address this complaint.

What does the Seventh Amendment's reference to "common law" mean?
The Constitution organized the government, providing power to act in certain areas and restricting actions in others. Common Law was inherited from England and remained in effect after the Constitution was adopted. Common Law defined the types of cases decided by juries, and reserved other cases for judges. The Seventh Amendment recognized this distinction.

Decisions reserved for judges were considered a different area of law, known as Equity. These types of cases included areas where parties were ordered to do or refrain from doing something (an injunction). Equity covered other issues including Family Law and Probate. The guiding force for the judge under the Rules of Equity was to be fair and just. Most areas of what was formerly known as Equity have been addressed by statute, but remain assigned to judges, not juries, for decision.

Why is there a special provision for "civil cases"?

The Seventh Amendment extends the right to a jury trial to federal civil cases such as car accidents, disputes between corporations for breach of contract, or most discrimination or employment disputes. In civil cases, the person bringing the lawsuit (the plaintiff) seeks money damages or a court order preventing the person being sued (the defendant) from engaging in certain conduct. To win, the plaintiff must prove his or her case by "a preponderance of the evidence," that is by over fifty percent of the proof.

Although the Seventh Amendment says it is limited to "suits at common law," meaning cases that triggered the right to a jury under English law, the amendment has been found to apply in lawsuits that are similar to the old common law cases. For example, the right to a jury trial applies to cases brought under federal statutes that prohibit race or gender discrimination in housing or employment. But importantly, the Seventh Amendment guarantees the right to a jury trial only in federal court, not in state court.

The 8th Amendment

Excessive bail shall not be required, nor excessive fines imposed, nor cruel and unusual punishments inflicted.

The Eighth Amendment: Ban on Cruel and Unusual Punishment

Excessive bail shall not be required, nor excessive fines imposed, nor cruel and unusual punishments inflicted.

What is the history and purpose of the Eighth Amendment?
The Eighth Amendment is a group of "procedural" rights designed to protect the inalienable right to liberty. It requires the government to follow certain rules if it attempts to interfere with liberty.

In 1641, The Massachusetts Bay Colony adopted a Body of Liberties with a right to bail and prohibiting cruel and inhuman punishments. The Eighth Amendment's language is virtually identical to the 1776 Virginia Declaration of Rights.

The 1776 Virginia provision was:

That excessive bail ought not to be required, nor excessive fines imposed, nor cruel and unusual punishments inflicted.

This is a small example of how important the colonial experience was in shaping the Bill of Rights.

A defendant's pre-trial detention is affected by the excessive bail clause. Excessive fines still have not been defined by the Supreme Court. Cruel and unusual punishment has been a major subject of many Eighth Amendment court cases, very often whether the death penalty is cruel and unusual.

Why is there a provision against excessive bail?

Bail is an amount of money that a person accused of a crime provides a court to be released before his trial. The prohibition against excessive bail protects an inalienable right not written in the Constitution, but is crucial to freedom and liberty.

A person accused of a crime is presumed innocent until found guilty at a trial or pleads guilty in open court. It is difficult to prepare a defense and consult with counsel while in custody and if he cannot reasonably gain his freedom, he is handicapped in defending his freedom.

Bail is excessive when set at an amount higher than necessary to ensure a defendant's appearance at trial, and if found guilty serve the sentence. Bail may not be set higher than needed to meet those ends.

Bail may only be denied when it has been demonstrated that the defendant is a danger to the community.

The Right to be Presumed Innocent is not written in the Constitution, but is a right that belongs to all of us.

What is an "excessive fine"?

The Supreme Court has not given definition to an excessive fine. In cases of indigents who may be imprisoned for failure to pay fines the Court has used the Equal Protection Clause of the Fourteenth Amendment to allow indigent defendants to go free and so has not addressed the amount of fines as excessive.

It is clear that large punitive damages in civil lawsuits are not covered by the Eighth Amendment. The Supreme Court has indicated that civil forfeiture proceedings where a person's property is taken by the government related to a criminal proceeding may be subject to the Excessive Fines Clause, but the answer to that question has not been definitive.

As a thought, what about the ever growing fines for traffic violations? Such fines might be excessive for those unable to pay and as a result lose their driving privileges. This has not been challenged under the Eighth Amendment, but perhaps it will be one day.

What types of punishment are "cruel and unusual"?

Some punishments are forbidden entirely by the Cruel and Unusual Punishments Clause. In 1878, while upholding a sentence that a convicted murderer be "publicly shot" in *Wilkerson v. Utah*, the Supreme Court provided examples of punishment that would be cruel and unusual punishment for any crime:

- Drawing and quartering
- Public dissecting
- Burning alive
- Disemboweling

Many of these had been punishments for crimes in England prior to the Revolution. The crime of treason in England specifically provided that each one of the above punishments would be inflicted. The Eighth Amendment made clear that the cruelty of the English was not to be copied by the new American federal government.

Is the death penalty "cruel and unusual"?

In 1972, the Supreme Court outlined a test to determine if the death penalty is banned by the Eighth Amendment in *Furman v. Georgia*. The elements of the test are:

- The "essential predicate" is "that a punishment must not by its severity be degrading to human dignity," especially torture.
- A severe punishment that is obviously inflicted in wholly arbitrary fashion.
- A severe punishment that is clearly and totally rejected throughout society.
- A severe punishment that is patently unnecessary.

The Court found that sentences of death were being imposed in an arbitrary fashion, and that the discretion and lack of direction given to judges and juries was resulting in some similarly situated defendants receiving death sentences while others did not. The Court determined this was "cruel and unusual." As a result, no executions took place over the next four years while states revised their capital punishment laws. Many of the revised laws provided for separate trials as to a defendant's guilt and a second "trial" regarding the appropriate penalty. The Supreme Court found such laws were not arbitrary in the 1976 case of *Gregg v. Georgia* and executions resumed.

On January 17, 1977, convicted murderer Gary Gilmore told a Utah firing squad, "Let's do it." and became the first prisoner executed under the new death penalty laws.

Has the Supreme Court ever ruled the death penalty to be cruel and unusual?

Though the death penalty is recognized in the Constitution and is not "cruel and unusual" generally in the Eighth Amendment sense, the Supreme Court has found that it offends the constitution in certain circumstances. In 1977, the Court found death was an inappropriate punishment for the crime of rape. In 1982, the Court found the death penalty unconstitutional when applied to someone convicted of "felony murder." In 2002, the Supreme Court determined that the execution of a mentally handicapped defendant was cruel and unusual. In 2005, the Supreme Court determined that the execution of a person who was younger than eighteen at the time the crime was committed was cruel and unusual.

The Ninth Amendment: Protection for Unenumerated Rights

The enumeration in the Constitution, of certain rights, shall not be construed to deny or disparage others retained by the people.

What are "unenumerated rights"?

The Ninth Amendment makes clear that the people have essential rights, beyond those listed in the First through Eighth Amendments. The Constitution's supporters had argued that it would be dangerous to list particular rights (such as free speech or the right to bear arms) as this left the impression that there were no rights other than those listed. This was the reason the unamended Constitution did not include a Bill of Rights. This argument was unacceptable to those wishing specific protections from a tyrannical government and a Bill of Rights was demanded. The Ninth Amendment was included to make clear the list was not complete.

Unlike the detailed list in the first eight amendments (and others that are listed in the unamended Constitution, e.g. the writ of "*habeas corpus*," rights protected by the Ninth Amendment are not listed with detail. The detailed rights are called "enumerated," hence Ninth Amendment rights are referred to as "unenumerated." These unenumerated rights include such important rights as the right to travel, the right to vote, the right to keep personal matters private and to make important decisions about one's health care or body.

What is the purpose of the Ninth Amendment?
The Ninth Amendment provides the basis for recognizing other, "unenumerated" rights, generally considered to arise from both natural law and the country's common law traditions. The import of the Ninth Amendment is that such rights exist and no constitutional grant of government power extinguished those rights.

It is straightforward and simple. The simplicity hides the deep meaning of the Ninth Amendment. It acknowledges that it is impossible to name all the rights that people possess to protect their lives and liberties and to pursue happiness. It is a direct statement that there are natural, inalienable rights that all people possess.

What types of rights are recognized by the Ninth Amendment?
There are many rights that are recognized in our society that are not named in the first eight amendments. If the Ninth Amendment did not exist, it might be argued that there was no constitutional protection for:

- The Right of Free Association
- The Right to the Presumption of Innocence
- The Right to a Fair Trial
- The Right to Privacy

These rights and others commonly recognized are never mentioned in the Constitution, but are accepted by the Supreme Court and society generally as having constitutional protection. This is consistent with the founding philosophy expressed in the Declaration of

Independence "that all men are created equal, that they are endowed by their Creator with certain unalienable Rights."

The Declaration enumerates the most fundamental rights of life, liberty and the pursuit of happiness. These are borrowed from the writings of John Locke, who is pictured at the beginning of this chapter.

Why was the Ninth Amendment needed?

The Ninth Amendment was needed because of a legal rule and the protections from government provided by the first eight Amendments. The Constitution is a legal document and many Founders were lawyers. Legal concerns came out of this rule: *"Expressio unius est exclusio alterius."* In English this means: *"the express mention of one thing excludes all others."*

The first eight amendments expressly mention rights like religion, speech, press and the bearing of arms. This became a problem in limiting the government. According to the rule, by mentioning limits on the government's power over those rights, meant the government would have power over any other "rights" that were not mentioned.

The Ninth Amendment addressed this problem by explicitly saying that just because rights were not named that did not mean the government was granted power to interfere with them. The Ninth Amendment was needed to "secure the blessings of liberty" for posterity.

The 10th Amendment

The powers not delegated to the United States by the Constitution, nor prohibited by it to the States, are reserved to the States respectively, or to the people.

The Tenth Amendment: Powers Reserved to the People and the States

The powers not delegated to the United States by the Constitution, nor prohibited by it to the States, are reserved to the States respectively, or to the people.

What is the purpose of the Tenth Amendment?

In the United States, state governments are granted power to make laws for the people within their borders. These powers come from the state constitutions. Simultaneously, the federal government, by virtue of the Constitution, makes laws for all the people in the country. This organization, with different governments having authority over the same territory is called federalism. The key to this arrangement is that the governments have power over different subjects. The idea of American Federalism is to protect freedom by limiting each government in its own area.

The federal government was intended to have only the powers listed in the Constitution, with any powers not listed left to the states as granted by their own constitutions. The Tenth Amendment was included to make this clear and to limit the federal government from overstepping its bounds.

What kinds of subjects did the Founders intend to be reserved to the powers of the states?

In various debates, writings and publications, the Federalists assured people that the states would retain power over most domestic issues, including, but not limited to:

- governance of religion
- training the militia and appointing militia officers
- control over local government
- most crimes and state justice systems
- family affairs
- real property titles and conveyances
- wills and inheritance
- the promotion of useful arts in ways other than granting patents and copyrights
- control of personal property outside of commerce
- the law of torts and contracts, except in suits between citizens of different states
- education
- services for the poor and unfortunate
- licensing of taverns
- roads other than post roads
- ferries and bridges
- regulation of fisheries, farms, and other business enterprises

This list is not all inclusive, and these matters were only the subject of state power if the people had granted such power through their state constitution. The expectation was that the federal government would exercise control ONLY over the subjects mentioned in Article I, Section 8. This reservation of powers to the states was seen as a protection against federal infringement upon the people's liberty.

What was another purpose of the Tenth Amendment?
This amendment was to answer concerns during the ratification process that the Constitution's central government would not usurp powers intended to remain with the States and the people. The key principle of the Constitution was originally quite simple: *positive grant of enumerated powers.*

Among the questions raised by opponents of the Constitution during the ratification debates was the lack of an express limit on federal power, and that the lack of the limit would be a danger to individual freedoms and to the powers of the states. The Tenth Amendment expressly added that limit.

The people appointed the federal government their agent for certain purposes and their own states for other purposes. The Tenth Amendment explains that the federal government is authorized to exercise *only* those powers which are specifically given to it. It makes clear the principles of federalism underlying the Constitution and the purpose of protecting freedom.

Which Founding Fathers were most responsible for the addition of the Tenth Amendment?

Adoption of the Constitution of 1787 was not a foregone conclusion. Ratification was opposed by a number of well-known patriots including Patrick Henry, Samuel Adams, and Thomas Jefferson. They argued that the Constitution would ultimately lead to a strong, centralized state with the power to be dangerous to the liberties won in the Revolution at so great a cost in blood and treasure. The Constitution's opponents became known as "Anti-Federalists." We owe a great debt for the protections afforded by the Bill of Rights to the opponents of the Constitution.

It was the influence and determination of the Constitution's opponents that resulted in the Tenth Amendment and the rest of the Bill of Rights.

The Tenth Amendment serves to emphasize the *limited nature* of the central government. The Tenth Amendment reinforces the understanding of the ratifiers that the states and the people, were to continue exercising power over all subjects that were not specifically placed under federal authority.

Why did Thomas Jefferson believe the Tenth Amendment was the foundation of the Constitution?

The Tenth Amendment makes explicit what the structure of the Constitution makes implicit. The implicit nature arose from the legal rule for reading documents: "*the express mention of one thing excludes all others.*" If authority was not delegated to the federal government via the Constitution and its enumerated powers, that authority did not belong to the federal government.

Since the real power resides in the people that power was reserved to the states if the people had granted the power in the state constitution. If the state was not given the power by the people, it remained with the people. While the logic of the Constitution leads to this conclusion, the Tenth Amendment states it clearly.

Thomas Jefferson considered the Tenth Amendment the "foundation" of the Constitution since the principle of the Tenth Amendment underpins the entire logic and meaning of the Constitution.

Epilogue

In the early twentieth century, a small, but politically important, eastern European country, Lithuania (near the Baltic Sea), was occupied by the Russian tsar's army. A young man and a girl who did not know each other lived in Lithuania.

The young man learned that the foreign tsar's army would soon be drafting him into its service. Aware that the Russian soldiers often brutally mistreated the conscripted Lithuanians; he did what many young Lithuania men did, by the thousands. He left his home for the hope of the United States.

A Self-Contained Community with Little Need for English

Over time he held many different jobs, including as a coal miner and a farm worker. On the farm he learned the skills of a butcher. He eventually put those skills to work in Chicago. In the early twentieth century, Chicago was home to a large Lithuanian community.

The community was essentially self-contained. There was a Lithuanian language newspaper *Draugas*, (which is still published today) and small shops, services and restaurants run by Lithuanian business owners. As the twentieth century began in Chicago, a Lithuanian could get along well with limited or no English skills.

Conflict across the Russian Empire Breaks Up a Family

Back in Lithuania, things were in turmoil. Across the Russian empire, people in occupied lands were revolting. In Lithuania, danger was ever present. No place was safe from the unrest, even the farm where the young girl lived with her large family of ten brothers and sisters. Armed conflict spread throughout Russia drawing ever closer to her home.

The family's concern for the safety of the youngest children grew daily. At her family's insistence, when she was fifteen, the girl boarded a ship, all alone, crossed the Atlantic with a hope for safety and security in America. She would be welcomed by extended family members in Boston. One sister and one brother would make it to the United States as well. The other eight were not so lucky. Over time, all would die at the hands of the occupiers.

A New Family Starts in America

The girl also made her way to Chicago's Lithuanian community. There she met the man who had fled the Russian draft. They fell in love, married, and had a son.

The boy grew up in Chicago, went to school, learned to read and write English, and studied American history. It became the practice for him to read the English language *Chicago Tribune* to his parents. At first he would translate from English to Lithuanian, but over time, it just became reading the English. He also shared with his parents his studies about the United States. From their son, the Lithuanian immigrants learned English and about the heritage of their new country.

Their son was the bridge for them. He not only translated the news, it fell to him unknowingly to translate AMERICA.

Not a Lithuanian Story, an American Story

Does the story of people fleeing a dangerous and oppressive place for the freedom, hope and safety of America sound familiar? Might such a story be part of your family history? If you reflect a bit you'll realize, while the story began in Lithuania, clearly it's not a Lithuanian story, it's an American story.

At some point in every American story, there is a generation that is the bridge. The people in the bridge generation not only translate the matters of daily life, they also serve to translate America. Whether the language is German, Dutch, Lithuanian or Spanish, the completion of these American stories always involves a translation of the principles that are the heritage of all Americans. The principles of The Declaration of Independence, Constitution and Bill of Rights that recognize the equality of people before the law, the purpose of government as a both servant of the people and protector of the rights of an individual are universal.

A Note from the Author

Early in my legal career I was an Assistant State's Attorney in Cook County, IL, primarily in criminal prosecutions. After I left the office, my work in private practice has been primarily in criminal defense. I mention this because the one place in law where issues surrounding the United States Constitution are a part of daily life is criminal justice. I've lived professionally with the Constitution daily for over twenty-five years.

The Founding Fathers were quite suspicious of government power. They had particular concerns about the power to imprison people. They had seen such power misused for political purposes. As a result, protections for the people against a tyrannical government throwing people into jail are found throughout the Constitution.

Limits on use of that power are in the original constitution with provisions for juries, *habeas corpus*, prohibiting government from making something a crime after an act has been committed or making a criminal law apply to one or a small group of people. The Bill of Rights is primarily related to matters of criminal justice. The First and Second Amendments' protections for expression and the right to bear arms limit the government's power to make the exercise of those rights a criminal act. The Fourth, Fifth, Sixth, and Eighth Amendments of the Bill of Rights provide protections for the life, liberty and property of someone accused of a crime.

A number of years ago, I began participating in Constitution Day presentations at high schools. (Constitution Day is September 17th, the day the Constitutional Convention completed its work in 1787). The experience surprised me. I was shocked by how little the students knew, and astounded that the teachers seemed to know only slightly more.

As a result I started writing about the Constitution for an online magazine. The responses and comments confirmed what I discovered at the high schools: there was very limited knowledge among Americans about their shared heritage of freedom. That was discouraging, but there was also an encouraging element to the comments.

While the comments demonstrated limited knowledge, they also showed a strong interest that led me to realize Americans had a thirst for a clear and thorough understanding of their rights under their Constitution. The guest writing turned into a personal website, shestokas.com, and the website into a radio show. The weekly show, *Constitutionally Speaking*, resulted in a short daily feature: "A Minute of Constitutionally Speaking." *Constitutional Sound Bites* developed from a collection of those minutes.

Read the "Sound Bites" Aloud

Though *Constitutional Sound Bites* is sorted into subject areas, each short piece is meant to stand on its own. The "minutes" range generally from 115 to 170 words.

While each can be read silently in less than a minute, if they are read aloud, like on the radio, the reading takes about a minute. I hope you'll try this. Hearing these ideas aloud is a different experience than reading them silently.

American Common Ground in the Constitution

The web site, the radio show, the daily feature and this book all have the same goal: to bring the Constitution alive and explain the origins, purposes and philosophy of the document. Reading the Constitution with the goals for government, as expressed in the Declaration of Independence and Preamble, in mind makes it more meaningful.

Knowledge of the goals reveals the purpose of the detailed provisions. Then the provisions are not simply dry definitions of government structure. They are protections for freedom and liberty.

Perhaps the most important thing to consider about the Declaration of Independence, the Constitution and the Bill of Rights is they are not Democrat or Republican, nor liberal or conservative, they are

American. Their ideals and principles belong to all of us, regardless of the language we speak.

Join my Facebook Group: Dave Shestokas on the Constitution

Follow me on Twitter: @Shestokas

Connect on LinkedIn: https://www.linkedin.com/in/davidshestokas

Visit my website: Constitutional and Legal Education and News

About David J. Shestokas

David Shestokas earned his Bachelor of Arts in Political Science from Bradley University and his Juris Doctor from The John Marshall Law School, cum laude, while serving on *The John Marshall Law Review*.

Additionally, he studied comparative legal systems at Trinity College in Dublin, Ireland. He has been admitted to practice law in both state and federal courts in Illinois and Florida.

As a prosecutor and criminal defense attorney for more than twenty-five years, he lived with the Constitution in the courtroom daily. As an Assistant State's Attorney for Cook County, IL he appeared in court on more than 10,000 criminal prosecutions. While on the Felony Review Unit, he participated in police investigations and made charging decisions in more than 400 felony cases.

In 1992, after the Republic of Lithuania regained its independence from the Soviet Union, Mr. Shestokas joined attorneys of Lithuanian heritage from around the world as a member of the First World Congress of Lithuanian Lawyers. The Lithuanian President, government officials, and the Lithuanian Bar worked with that Congress to restore the rule of law and a constitutional government after four generations of Soviet occupation.

Mr. Shestokas is the author of the series, *Constitutional Sound Bites*, which grew from his weekly radio show, *Constitutionally Speaking*, and his website, Constitutional Legal Education and News. The website has more than 350,000 annual visitors. His readership is balanced across partisan, economic, ethnic and philosophical persuasions. He resonates with today's readers, be they scholars, teachers, young students, immigrants, history buffs, or the general public, as his style is direct and easy to understand in twenty-first century phrasing; while retaining the integrity of the American Founders.

Along with volunteering at the Salvation Army providing *pro bono* legal services for the homeless, David has also given his time at the Quality Life Center to educate at-risk youth about the values ingrained in America's Founding.

Mr. Shestokas' current project is collaborating with Dr. Berta Arias, past President, Illinois Latino Council on Higher Education to provide accurate Spanish language materials on the constitutional heritage of the United States.

About Berta Isabel Arias*

Berta Arias, Ed.D., is an accomplished Cuban-America woman of many talents and the recipient of numerous awards garnered during an illustrious career as a professor in world languages and international education in the Chicago area. She is passionate about everyone and everything to whom and to which she lends her time and attention. Dr. Arias has made helping others, saving communities and bringing beauty and learning through the arts a cornerstone of her being.

She served as the first Board President of the Illinois Latino Council on Higher Education, (ILACHE) where she has funded a scholarship for Excellence in Writing. Not satisfied with giving just financial support, Dr. Arias offers the winning students her personal time to help them achieve their goals. In her collaboration with Dave Shestokas, Esq., on Constitutional Sound Bites, she lends her extensive experience in translation toward those same goals of helping young Latinos succeed in America.

---

* Dr. Arias's contribution beyond translations for *Cápsulas Informativas Constitucionales* was invaluable. The final rendition of *Constitutional Sound Bites* included more material than the originals because of her input during the process involved in creating the Spanish. DJS

Throughout her academic career, Dr. Arias has channeled her creativity by writing poetry and short stories. Now on her next stage of life, she has moved to Amelia Island, Florida. There, when she is not championing the cause of trees, the environment, libraries and education, she revels in writing novels.

Her first book, *Mango Rain*, is a luscious story of intrigue, beauty and love that spans Chicago and Havana. Its prequel, *Mimi's Path*, is due out spring 2016.

Visit Dr. Arias at her website: www.bertaariasauthor.com

Acknowledgements

No book is the creation of a single person. *Constitutional Sound Bites* and *Cápsulas Informativas Constitucionales* are no exception.

As this English collection of *Constitutional Sound Bites* was completed after the development of the Spanish *Cápsulas Informativas Constitucionales,* the story of that book is the place to start.

The story of *Cápsulas Informativas Constitucionales* truly starts more than fifteen years ago when my wife Elaine proposed that we study Spanish. We took a course together, and to practice our Spanish we attended Spanish language mass and have Sunday breakfast in the Chicago's Mexican-American neighborhood known as Little Village. Without Elaine's ongoing interest in the Spanish language and Latino culture there would never have been *Cápsulas Informativas Constitucionales.*

Elaine continued her Spanish studies with courses taught by Dr. Berta Arias. As a result of those classes, we joined a group organized by Dr. Arias that traveled to Cuba to study language and culture. During that trip to Cuba, Dr. Arias and I formed a friendship. That friendship would result in the collaboration to produce this work. That collaboration was invaluable in the creation of *Cápsulas Informativas*. Dr. Arias did much more than translate. As her translation work progressed we consulted regularly. As a result this book does not simply translate my original writings, but also the eighteenth century English and legal terms of the Founding Documents to represent in Spanish the essence of America's founding principles. Without Dr. Arias' knowledge of the languages and Latino culture this book would not exist.

All along the way, since the beginning of this project, from first meeting with Dr. Arias to discuss the project to the final draft, Jill

Horist has been a part of *Cápsulas Informativas Constitucionales* and *Constitutional Sound Bites.*

Thanks to Turning Point USA, an organization dedicated to teaching American principles to high school and college students around the country. In July, 2015, Turning Point hosted a Young Latino Leadership Summit. At the summit, I was given the chance to speak with fifty young Latino leaders from around the country about this project, and the input I received was important in decisions about what should be included in this book.

Veronica Culbertson of the Southwest Florida Hispanic Chamber of Commerce and Javier Fuller and Ingrid Molina of Fuller Online Solutions also shared thoughts important to content. Jameson Campaigne of Jameson Books provided invaluable technical assistance. Dr. Heather Downey and William Frech provided editorial assistance. Jon Patch of America's Talk Radio Network first proposed the idea of the short radio features that would lead to these books. Paul Romanowski of PDR Designs gave life to the idea of the Founding Fathers in headphones. Charles King of Cox-King Multimedia is thanked for his patience and professionalism in creating the final presentations in two languages.

Finally, thanks to America's Founders and to my grandparents, Barbara and John Shestokas, who came to America from Lithuania.

Notes About *Cápsulas Informativas Constitucionales*

(Translation in Spanish by Berta Isabel Arias of *Constitutional Sound Bites* by David J. Shestokas)*

The founding documents here cited in Spanish (the Declaration of Independence, the Constitution and the Bill of Rights) were translated by various agencies and the reader of *Cápsulas Informativas Constitucionales* will quickly notice the difference in the translation of some phrases and words between the agencies' quotes and the same phrases and words in *Cápsulas Informativas Constitucionales*.

You will see, for example, that the cited translation says "Tribunal Supremo" and in *Cápsulas Informativas Constitucionales* we say "la Corte Suprema," "los Estados Unidos" in the quote and in Cápsulas Informativas Constitucionales, "Estados Unidos." This translation maintains grammatical integrity while integrating the modern use of these phrases.

The last note that merits mentioning here for the reader is that given the close working collaboration that we have maintained throughout this project, *Cápsulas Informativas Constitucionales* faithfully captures David Shestokas's voice in *Constitutional Sound Bites*. The result, therefore, is that whether read in English or Spanish, the information contained in these works about the constitutional heritage of the United States is the same and, I trust, will have the same impact on the reader.

—Berta Isabel Arias

---

* This information originally appeared in the Spanish edition of this work. It is included here for two reasons. First is to call attention to the English reader the care that was taken to translate not just words, but to accurately express in Spanish concepts critical to America's Founding. The second is to meet a goal of having the English and Spanish editions mirror each other to provide readers of differing skill levels in either language wishing to discuss the ideas with others the tools to easily do so. DJS

The Declaration of Independence

IN CONGRESS, July 4, 1776.
The unanimous Declaration of the thirteen united States of America

When in the Course of human events, it becomes necessary for one people to dissolve the political bands which have connected them with another, and to assume among the powers of the earth, the separate and equal station to which the Laws of Nature and of Nature's God entitle them, a decent respect to the opinions of mankind requires that they should declare the causes which impel them to the separation.

We hold these truths to be self-evident, that all men are created equal, that they are endowed by their Creator with certain unalienable Rights, that among these are Life, Liberty and the pursuit of Happiness.—That to secure these rights, Governments are instituted among Men, deriving their just powers from the consent of the governed, —That whenever any Form of Government becomes destructive of these ends, it is the Right of the People to alter or to abolish it, and to institute new Government, laying its foundation on such principles and organizing its powers in such form, as to them shall seem most likely to effect their Safety and Happiness. Prudence, indeed, will dictate that Governments long established should not be changed for light and transient causes; and accordingly all experience hath shewn, that mankind are more disposed to suffer, while evils are sufferable, than to right themselves by abolishing the forms to which they are accustomed. But when a long train of abuses and usurpations, pursuing invariably the same Object evinces a design to reduce them under absolute Despotism, it is their right, it is their duty, to throw off such Government, and to provide new Guards for their future security.—Such has been the patient sufferance of these Colonies; and such is now the necessity which constrains them to alter their former Systems of Government. The history of the present King of Great Britain is a history of repeated injuries and usurpations, all having in direct object the establishment of an absolute Tyranny over these States. To prove this, let Facts be submitted to a candid world.

He has refused his Assent to Laws, the most wholesome and necessary for the public good. He has forbidden his Governors to pass Laws of immediate and pressing importance, unless suspended in their operation till his Assent should be obtained; and when so suspended, he has utterly neglected to attend to them. He has refused to pass other Laws for the accommodation of large districts of people, unless those people would relinquish the right of Representation in the Legislature, a right inestimable to them and formidable to tyrants only. He has called together legislative bodies at places unusual, uncomfortable, and distant from the depository of their public Records, for the sole purpose of fatiguing them into compliance with his measures. He has dissolved Representative Houses repeatedly, for opposing with manly firmness his invasions on the rights of the people. He has refused for a long time, after such dissolutions, to cause others to be elected; whereby the Legislative powers, incapable of Annihilation, have returned to the People at large for their exercise; the State remaining in the mean time exposed to all the dangers of invasion from without, and convulsions within. He has endeavoured to prevent the population of these States; for that purpose obstructing the Laws for Naturalization of Foreigners; refusing to pass others to encourage their migrations hither, and raising the conditions of new Appropriations of Lands. He has obstructed the Administration of Justice, by refusing his Assent to Laws for establishing Judiciary powers. He has made Judges dependent on his Will alone, for the tenure of their offices, and the amount and payment of their salaries. He has erected a multitude of New Offices, and sent hither swarms of Officers to harrass our people, and eat out their substance. He has kept among us, in times of peace, Standing Armies without the Consent of our legislatures. He has affected to render the Military independent of and superior to the Civil power. He has combined with others to subject us to a jurisdiction foreign to our constitution, and unacknowledged by our laws; giving his Assent to their Acts of pretended Legislation: For Quartering large bodies of armed troops among us: For protecting them, by a mock Trial, from punishment for any Murders which they should commit on the Inhabitants of these States: For cutting off our Trade with all parts of the world: For imposing Taxes on us without our Consent: For depriving us in many cases, of the benefits of Trial by Jury: For transporting us beyond Seas to be tried for pretended offences For abolishing the free System of English Laws in a neighbouring Province, establishing therein an Arbitrary government, and enlarging its Boundaries so as to render it at once an example and fit instrument for introducing the same absolute rule into these Colonies: For taking away our Charters, abolishing our most valuable Laws, and altering fundamentally the Forms of our Governments: For suspending our own Legislatures, and declaring themselves invested with power to legislate for us in all cases whatsoever. He has abdicated Government here, by declaring us out of his Protection and waging War against us. He has plundered our seas, ravaged our Coasts, burnt our towns, and destroyed the lives of our people. He is at this time transporting large Armies of foreign Mercenaries to compleat the works of death, desolation and tyranny, already begun with circumstances of Cruelty & perfidy scarcely paralleled in the most barbarous ages, and totally unworthy the Head of a civilized nation. He has constrained our fellow Citizens taken Captive on the high Seas to bear Arms against their Country, to become the executioners of their friends and Brethren, or to fall themselves by their Hands. He has excited domestic insurrections amongst us, and has endeavoured to bring on the inhabitants of our frontiers, the merciless Indian Savages, whose known rule of warfare, is an undistinguished destruction of all ages, sexes and conditions.

In every stage of these Oppressions We have Petitioned for Redress in the most humble terms: Our repeated Petitions have been answered only by repeated injury. A Prince whose character is thus marked by every act which may define a Tyrant, is unfit to be the ruler of a free people.

Nor have We been wanting in attentions to our British brethren. We have warned them from time to time of attempts by their legislature to extend an unwarrantable jurisdiction over us. We have reminded them of the circumstances of our emigration and settlement here. We have appealed to their native justice and magnanimity, and we have conjured them by the ties of our common kindred to disavow these usurpations, which, would inevitably interrupt our connections and correspondence. They too have been deaf to the voice of justice and of consanguinity. We must, therefore, acquiesce in the necessity, which denounces our Separation, and hold them, as we hold the rest of mankind, Enemies in War, in Peace Friends.

We, therefore, the Representatives of the united States of America, in General Congress, Assembled, appealing to the Supreme Judge of the world for the rectitude of our intentions, do, in the Name, and by Authority of the good People of these Colonies, solemnly publish and declare, That these United Colonies are, and of Right ought to be Free and Independent States; that they are Absolved from all Allegiance to the British Crown, and that all political connection between them and the State of Great Britain, is and ought to be totally dissolved; and that as Free and Independent States, they have full Power to levy War, conclude Peace, contract Alliances, establish Commerce, and to do all other Acts and Things which Independent States may of right do. And for the support of this Declaration, with a firm reliance on the protection of divine Providence, we mutually pledge to each other our Lives, our Fortunes and our sacred Honor.

John Hancock

. . .

. . .

New Hampshire: Josiah Bartlett, William Whipple, Matthew Thornton

Massachusetts: Samuel Adams, John Adams, John Hancock, Robert Treat Paine, Elbridge Gerry

Rhode Island: Stephen Hopkins, William Ellery

Connecticut: Roger Sherman, Samuel Huntington, William Williams, Oliver Wolcott

New York: William Floyd, Philip Livingston, Francis Lewis, Lewis Morris

New Jersey: Richard Stockton, John Witherspoon, Francis Hopkinson, John Hart, Abraham Clark

Pennsylvania: Robert Morris, Benjamin Rush, Benjamin Franklin, John Morton, George Clymer, James Smith, George Taylor, James Wilson, George Ross

Delaware: George Read, Caesar Rodney, Thomas McKean

Maryland: Samuel Chase, William Paca, Thomas Stone, Charles Carroll of Carrollton

Virginia: George Wythe, Richard Henry Lee, Thomas Jefferson, Benjamin Harrison, Thomas Nelson, Jr., Francis Lightfoot Lee, Carter Braxton

North Carolina: William Hooper, Joseph Hewes, John Penn

South Carolina: Edward Rutledge, Thomas Heyward, Jr., Thomas Lynch, Jr., Arthur Middleton

Georgia: Button Gwinnett, Lyman Hall, George Walton

The Constitution
of the United States of America

WE THE PEOPLE of the United States, in Order to form a more perfect Union, establish Justice, insure domestic Tranquility, provide for the common defence, promote the general Welfare, and secure the Blessings of Liberty to ourselves and our Posterity, do ordain and establish this Constitution for the United States of America.

Article. I.
Section. 1.
All legislative Powers herein granted shall be vested in a Congress of the United States, which shall consist of a Senate and House of Representatives.

Section. 2.
The House of Representatives shall be composed of Members chosen every second Year by the People of the several States, and the Electors in each State shall have the Qualifications requisite for Electors of the most numerous Branch of the State Legislature.

No Person shall be a Representative who shall not have attained to the Age of twenty five Years, and been seven Years a Citizen of the United States, and who shall not, when elected, be an Inhabitant of that State in which he shall be chosen.

Representatives and direct Taxes shall be apportioned among the several States which may be included within this Union, according to their respective Numbers, which shall be determined by adding to the whole Number of free Persons, including those bound to Service for a Term of Years, and excluding Indians not taxed, three fifths of all other Persons. The actual Enumeration shall be made within three Years after the first Meeting of the Congress of the United States, and within every subsequent Term of ten Years, in such Manner as they shall by Law direct. The Number of Representatives shall not exceed one for every thirty Thousand, but each State shall have at Least one Representative; and until such enumeration shall be made, the State of New Hampshire shall be entitled to chuse three, Massachusetts eight, Rhode-Island and Providence Plantations one, Connecticut five, New-York six, New Jersey four, Pennsylvania eight, Delaware one, Maryland six, Virginia ten, North Carolina five, South Carolina five, and Georgia three.

When vacancies happen in the Representation from any State, the Executive Authority thereof shall issue Writs of Election to fill such Vacancies.

The House of Representatives shall chuse their Speaker and other Officers; and shall have the sole Power of Impeachment.

Section. 3.
The Senate of the United States shall be composed of two Senators from each State, chosen by the Legislature thereof for six Years; and each Senator shall have one Vote.

Immediately after they shall be assembled in Consequence of the first Election, they shall be divided as equally as may be into three Classes. The Seats of the Senators of the first Class shall be vacated at the Expiration of the second Year, of the second Class at the Expiration of the fourth Year, and of the third Class at the Expiration of the sixth Year, so that one third may be chosen every second Year; and if Vacancies happen by Resignation, or otherwise, during the Recess of the Legislature of any State, the Executive thereof may make temporary Appointments until the next Meeting of the Legislature, which shall then fill such Vacancies.

No Person shall be a Senator who shall not have attained to the Age of thirty Years, and been nine Years a Citizen of the United States, and who shall not, when elected, be an Inhabitant of that State for which he shall be chosen.

The Vice President of the United States shall be President of the Senate, but shall have no Vote, unless they be equally divided.

The Senate shall chuse their other Officers, and also a President pro tempore, in the Absence of the Vice President, or when he shall exercise the Office of President of the United States.

The Senate shall have the sole Power to try all Impeachments. When sitting for that Purpose, they shall be on Oath or Affirmation. When the President of the United States is tried, the Chief Justice shall preside: And no Person shall be convicted without the Concurrence of two thirds of the Members present.

Judgment in Cases of Impeachment shall not extend further than to removal from Office, and disqualification to hold and enjoy any Office of honor, Trust or Profit under the United States: but the Party convicted shall nevertheless be liable and subject to Indictment, Trial, Judgment and Punishment, according to Law.

Section. 4.

The Times, Places and Manner of holding Elections for Senators and Representatives, shall be prescribed in each State by the Legislature thereof; but the Congress may at any time by Law make or alter such Regulations, except as to the Places of chusing Senators.

The Congress shall assemble at least once in every Year, and such Meeting shall be on the first Monday in December, unless they shall by Law appoint a different Day.

Section. 5.

Each House shall be the Judge of the Elections, Returns and Qualifications of its own Members, and a Majority of each shall constitute a Quorum to do Business; but a smaller Number may adjourn from day to day, and may be authorized to compel the Attendance of absent Members, in such Manner, and under such Penalties as each House may provide.

Each House may determine the Rules of its Proceedings, punish its Members for disorderly Behaviour, and, with the Concurrence of two thirds, expel a Member.

Each House shall keep a Journal of its Proceedings, and from time to time publish the same, excepting such Parts as may in their Judgment require Secrecy; and the Yeas and Nays of the Members of either House on any question shall, at the Desire of one fifth of those Present, be entered on the Journal.

Neither House, during the Session of Congress, shall, without the Consent of the other, adjourn for more than three days, nor to any other Place than that in which the two Houses shall be sitting.

Section. 6.

The Senators and Representatives shall receive a Compensation for their Services, to be ascertained by Law, and paid out of the Treasury of the United States. They shall in all Cases, except Treason, Felony and Breach of the Peace, be privileged from Arrest during their Attendance at the Session of their respective Houses, and in going to and returning from the same; and for any Speech or Debate in either House, they shall not be questioned in any other Place.

No Senator or Representative shall, during the Time for which he was elected, be appointed to any civil Office under the Authority of the United States, which shall have been created, or the Emoluments whereof shall have been encreased during such time; and no Person holding any Office under the United States, shall be a Member of either House during his Continuance in Office.

Section. 7.

All Bills for raising Revenue shall originate in the House of Representatives; but the Senate may propose or concur with Amendments as on other Bills.

Every Bill which shall have passed the House of Representatives and the Senate, shall, before it become a Law, be presented to the President of the United States: If he approve he shall sign it, but if not he shall return it, with his Objections to that House in which it shall have originated, who shall enter the Objections at large on their Journal, and proceed to reconsider it. If after such Reconsideration two thirds of that House shall agree to pass the Bill, it shall be sent, together with the Objections, to the other House, by which it shall likewise be reconsidered, and if approved by two thirds of that House, it shall become a Law. But in all such Cases the Votes of both Houses shall be determined by yeas and Nays, and the Names of the Persons voting for and against the Bill shall be entered on the Journal of each House respectively. If any Bill shall not be returned by the President within ten Days (Sundays excepted) after it shall have been presented to him, the Same shall be a Law, in like Manner as if he had signed it, unless the Congress by their Adjournment prevent its Return, in which Case it shall not be a Law.

Every Order, Resolution, or Vote to which the Concurrence of the Senate and House of Representatives may be necessary (except on a question of Adjournment) shall be presented to the President of the United States; and before the Same shall take Effect, shall be approved by him, or being disapproved by him, shall be repassed by two thirds of the Senate and House of Representatives, according to the Rules and Limitations prescribed in the Case of a Bill.

Section. 8.

The Congress shall have Power To lay and collect Taxes, Duties, Imposts and Excises, to pay the Debts and provide for the common Defence and general Welfare of the United States; but all Duties, Imposts and Excises shall be uniform throughout the United States;

To borrow Money on the credit of the United States;

To regulate Commerce with foreign Nations, and among the several States, and with the Indian Tribes;

To establish an uniform Rule of Naturalization, and uniform Laws on the subject of Bankruptcies throughout the United States;

To coin Money, regulate the Value thereof, and of foreign Coin, and fix the Standard of Weights and Measures;

To provide for the Punishment of counterfeiting the Securities and current Coin of the United States;

To establish Post Offices and post Roads;

To promote the Progress of Science and useful Arts, by securing for limited Times to Authors and Inventors the exclusive Right to their respective Writings and Discoveries;

To constitute Tribunals inferior to the supreme Court;

To define and punish Piracies and Felonies committed on the high Seas, and Offences against the Law of Nations;

To declare War, grant Letters of Marque and Reprisal, and make Rules concerning Captures on Land and Water;

To raise and support Armies, but no Appropriation of Money to that Use shall be for a longer Term than two Years;

To provide and maintain a Navy;

To make Rules for the Government and Regulation of the land and naval Forces;

To provide for calling forth the Militia to execute the Laws of the Union, suppress Insurrections and repel Invasions;

To provide for organizing, arming, and disciplining, the Militia, and for governing such Part of them as may be employed in the Service of the United States, reserving to the States respectively, the Appointment of the Officers, and the Authority of training the Militia according to the discipline prescribed by Congress;

To exercise exclusive Legislation in all Cases whatsoever, over such District (not exceeding ten Miles square) as may, by Cession of particular States, and the Acceptance of Congress, become the Seat of the Government of the United States, and to exercise like Authority over all Places purchased by the Consent of the Legislature of the State in which the Same shall be, for the Erection of Forts, Magazines, Arsenals, dock-Yards, and other needful Buildings;—And

To make all Laws which shall be necessary and proper for carrying into Execution the foregoing Powers, and all other Powers vested by this Constitution in the Government of the United States, or in any Department or Officer thereof.

Section. 9.

The Migration or Importation of such Persons as any of the States now existing shall think proper to admit, shall not be prohibited by the Congress prior to the Year one thousand eight hundred and eight, but a Tax or duty may be imposed on such Importation, not exceeding ten dollars for each Person.

The Privilege of the Writ of Habeas Corpus shall not be suspended, unless when in Cases of Rebellion or Invasion the public Safety may require it.

No Bill of Attainder or ex post facto Law shall be passed.

No Capitation, or other direct, Tax shall be laid, unless in Proportion to the Census or enumeration herein before directed to be taken.

No Tax or Duty shall be laid on Articles exported from any State.

No Preference shall be given by any Regulation of Commerce or Revenue to the Ports of one State over those of another; nor shall Vessels bound to, or from, one State, be obliged to enter, clear, or pay Duties in another.

No Money shall be drawn from the Treasury, but in Consequence of Appropriations made by Law; and a regular Statement and Account of the Receipts and Expenditures of all public Money shall be published from time to time.

No Title of Nobility shall be granted by the United States: And no Person holding any Office of Profit or Trust under them, shall, without the Consent of the Congress, accept of any present, Emolument, Office, or Title, of any kind whatever, from any King, Prince, or foreign State.

Section. 10.

No State shall enter into any Treaty, Alliance, or Confederation; grant Letters of Marque and Reprisal; coin Money; emit Bills of Credit; make any Thing but gold and silver Coin a Tender in Payment of Debts; pass any Bill of Attainder, ex post facto Law, or Law impairing the Obligation of Contracts, or grant any Title of Nobility. No State shall, without the Consent of the Congress, lay any Imposts or Duties on Imports or Exports, except what may be absolutely necessary for executing it's inspection Laws: and the net Produce of all Duties and Imposts, laid by any State on Imports or Exports, shall be for the Use of the Treasury of the United States; and all such Laws shall be subject to the Revision and Controul of the Congress.

No State shall, without the Consent of Congress, lay any Duty of Tonnage, keep Troops, or Ships of War in time of Peace, enter into any Agreement or Compact with another State, or with a foreign Power, or engage in War, unless actually invaded, or in such imminent Danger as will not admit of delay.

Article. II.

Section. 1.

The executive Power shall be vested in a President of the United States of America. He shall hold his Office during the Term of four Years, and, together with the Vice President, chosen for the same Term, be elected, as follows:

Each State shall appoint, in such Manner as the Legislature thereof may direct, a Number of Electors, equal to the whole Number of Senators and Representatives to which the State may be entitled in the Congress: but no Senator or Representative, or Person holding an Office of Trust or Profit under the United States, shall be appointed an Elector.

The Electors shall meet in their respective States, and vote by Ballot for two Persons, of whom one at least shall not be an Inhabitant of the same State with themselves. And they shall make a List of all the Persons voted for, and of the Number of Votes for each; which List they shall sign and certify, and transmit sealed to the Seat of the Government of the United States, directed to the President of the Senate. The President of the Senate shall, in the Presence of the Senate and House of Representatives, open all the Certificates, and the Votes shall then be counted. The Person having the greatest Number of Votes shall be the President, if such Number be a Majority of the whole Number of Electors appointed; and if there be more than one who have such Majority, and have an equal Number of Votes, then the House of Representatives shall immediately chuse by Ballot one of them for President; and if no Person have a Majority, then from the five highest on the List the said House shall in like Manner chuse the President. But in chusing the President, the Votes shall be taken by States, the Representation from each State having one Vote; A quorum for this purpose shall consist of a Member or Members from two thirds of the States, and a Majority of all the States shall be necessary to a Choice. In every Case, after the Choice of the President, the Person having the greatest Number of Votes of the Electors shall be the Vice President. But if there should remain two or more who have equal Votes, the Senate shall chuse from them by Ballot the Vice President.

The Congress may determine the Time of chusing the Electors, and the Day on which they shall give their Votes; which Day shall be the same throughout the United States.

No Person except a natural born Citizen, or a Citizen of the United States, at the time of the Adoption of this Constitution, shall be eligible to the Office of President; neither shall any Person be eligible to that Office who shall not have attained to the Age of thirty five Years, and been fourteen Years a Resident within the United States.

In Case of the Removal of the President from Office, or of his Death, Resignation, or Inability to discharge the Powers and Duties of the said Office, the Same shall devolve on the Vice President, and the Congress may by Law provide for the Case of Removal, Death, Resignation or Inability, both of the President and Vice President, declaring what Officer shall then act as President, and such Officer shall act accordingly, until the Disability be removed, or a President shall be elected.

The President shall, at stated Times, receive for his Services, a Compensation, which shall neither be increased nor diminished during the Period for which he shall have been elected, and he shall not receive within that Period any other Emolument from the United States, or any of them.

Before he enter on the Execution of his Office, he shall take the following Oath or Affirmation:—"I do solemnly swear (or affirm) that I will faithfully execute the Office of President of the United States, and will to the best of my Ability, preserve, protect and defend the Constitution of the United States."

Section. 2.

The President shall be Commander in Chief of the Army and Navy of the United States, and of the Militia of the several States, when called into the actual Service of the United States; he may require the Opinion, in writing, of the principal Officer in each of the executive Departments, upon any Subject relating to the Duties of their respective Offices, and he shall have Power to grant Reprieves and Pardons for Offences against the United States, except in Cases of Impeachment.

He shall have Power, by and with the Advice and Consent of the Senate, to make Treaties, provided two thirds of the Senators present concur; and he shall nominate, and by and with the Advice and Consent of the Senate, shall appoint Ambassadors, other public Ministers and Consuls, Judges of the supreme Court, and all other Officers of the United States, whose Appointments are not herein otherwise provided for, and which shall be established by Law: but the Congress may by Law vest the Appointment of such inferior Officers, as they think proper, in the President alone, in the Courts of Law, or in the Heads of Departments.

The President shall have Power to fill up all Vacancies that may happen during the Recess of the Senate, by granting Commissions which shall expire at the End of their next Session.

Section. 3.

He shall from time to time give to the Congress Information of the State of the Union, and recommend to their Consideration such Measures as he shall judge necessary and expedient; he may, on extraordinary Occasions, convene both Houses, or either of them, and in Case of Disagreement between them, with Respect to the Time of Adjournment, he may adjourn them to such Time as he shall think proper; he shall receive Ambassadors and other public Ministers; he shall take Care that the Laws be faithfully executed, and shall Commission all the Officers of the United States.

Section. 4.

The President, Vice President and all civil Officers of the United States, shall be removed from Office on Impeachment for, and Conviction of, Treason, Bribery, or other high Crimes and Misdemeanors.

Article III.
Section. 1.

The judicial Power of the United States shall be vested in one supreme Court, and in such inferior Courts as the Congress may from time to time ordain and establish. The Judges, both of the supreme and inferior Courts, shall hold their Offices during good Behaviour, and shall, at stated Times, receive for their Services a Compensation, which shall not be diminished during their Continuance in Office.

Section. 2.

The judicial Power shall extend to all Cases, in Law and Equity, arising under this Constitution, the Laws of the

United States, and Treaties made, or which shall be made, under their Authority;—to all Cases affecting

Ambassadors, other public Ministers and Consuls;—to all Cases of admiralty and maritime Jurisdiction;—to Controversies to which the United States shall be a Party;—to Controversies between two or more States;— between a State and Citizens of another State,—between Citizens of different States,—between Citizens of the same State claiming Lands under Grants of different States, and between a State, or the Citizens thereof, and foreign States, Citizens or Subjects.

In all Cases affecting Ambassadors, other public Ministers and Consuls, and those in which a State shall be Party, the supreme Court shall have original Jurisdiction. In all the other Cases before mentioned, the supreme Court shall have appellate Jurisdiction, both as to Law and Fact, with such Exceptions, and under such Regulations as the Congress shall make.

The Trial of all Crimes, except in Cases of Impeachment, shall be by Jury; and such Trial shall be held in the State where the said Crimes shall have been committed; but when not committed within any State, the Trial shall be at such Place or Places as the Congress may by Law have directed.

Section. 3.

Treason against the United States, shall consist only in levying War against them, or in adhering to their Enemies, giving them Aid and Comfort. No Person shall be convicted of Treason unless on the Testimony of two Witnesses to the same overt Act, or on Confession in open Court.

The Congress shall have Power to declare the Punishment of Treason, but no Attainder of Treason shall work Corruption of Blood, or Forfeiture except during the Life of the Person attainted.

Article. IV.

Section. 1.

Full Faith and Credit shall be given in each State to the public Acts, Records, and judicial Proceedings of every other State. And the Congress may by general Laws prescribe the Manner in which such Acts, Records and Proceedings shall be proved, and the Effect thereof.

Section. 2.

The Citizens of each State shall be entitled to all Privileges and Immunities of Citizens in the several States.

A Person charged in any State with Treason, Felony, or other Crime, who shall flee from Justice, and be found in another State, shall on Demand of the executive Authority of the State from which he fled, be delivered up, to be removed to the State having Jurisdiction of the Crime.

No Person held to Service or Labour in one State, under the Laws thereof, escaping into another, shall, in Consequence of any Law or Regulation therein, be discharged from such Service or Labour, but shall be delivered up on Claim of the Party to whom such Service or Labour may be due.

Section. 3.

New States may be admitted by the Congress into this Union; but no new State shall be formed or erected within the Jurisdiction of any other State; nor any State be formed by the Junction of two or more States, or Parts of States, without the Consent of the Legislatures of the States concerned as well as of the Congress.

The Congress shall have Power to dispose of and make all needful Rules and Regulations respecting the Territory or other Property belonging to the United States; and nothing in this Constitution shall be so construed as to Prejudice any Claims of the United States, or of any particular State.

Section. 4.

The United States shall guarantee to every State in this Union a Republican Form of Government, and shall protect each of them against Invasion; and on Application of the Legislature, or of the Executive (when the Legislature cannot be convened), against domestic Violence.

Article. V.

The Congress, whenever two thirds of both Houses shall deem it necessary, shall propose Amendments to this

Constitution, or, on the Application of the Legislatures of two thirds of the several States, shall call a Convention for proposing Amendments, which, in either Case, shall be valid to all Intents and Purposes, as Part of this Constitution, when ratified by the Legislatures of three fourths of the several States, or by Conventions in three fourths thereof, as the one or the other Mode of Ratification may be proposed by the Congress; Provided that no Amendment which may be made prior to the Year One thousand eight hundred and eight shall in any Manner affect the first and fourth Clauses in the Ninth Section of the first Article; and that no State, without its Consent, shall be deprived of its equal Suffrage in the Senate.

Article. VI.

All Debts contracted and Engagements entered into, before the Adoption of this Constitution, shall be as valid against the United States under this Constitution, as under the Confederation.

This Constitution, and the Laws of the United States which shall be made in Pursuance thereof; and all Treaties made, or which shall be made, under the Authority of the United States, shall be the supreme Law of the Land; and the Judges in every State shall be bound thereby, any Thing in the Constitution or Laws of any State to the Contrary notwithstanding.

The Senators and Representatives before mentioned, and the Members of the several State Legislatures, and all executive and judicial Officers, both of the United States and of the several States, shall be bound by Oath or Affirmation, to support this Constitution; but no religious Test shall ever be required as a Qualification to any Office or public Trust under the United States.

Article. VII.

The Ratification of the Conventions of nine States, shall be sufficient for the Establishment of this Constitution between the States so ratifying the Same. Attest William Jackson Secretary done in Convention by the Unanimous Consent of the States present the Seventeenth Day of September in the Year of our Lord one thousand seven hundred and Eighty seven and of the Independance of the United States of America the Twelfth In witness whereof We have hereunto subscribed our Names,

G°. Washington, *Presidt and deputy from Virginia*

. . .

Amendments to the Constitution of the United States of America

ARTICLES in addition to, and Amendment of the Constitution of the United States of America, proposed by Congress, and ratified by the Legislatures of the several States, pursuant to the fifth Article of the original Constitution.

AMENDMENT I

Congress shall make no law respecting an establishment of religion, or prohibiting the free exercise thereof; or abridging the freedom of speech, or of the press; or the right of the people peaceably to assemble, and to petition the Government for a redress of grievances.

AMENDMENT II

A well regulated Militia, being necessary to the security of a free State, the right of the people to keep and bear Arms, shall not be infringed.

AMENDMENT III

No Soldier shall, in time of peace be quartered in any house, without the consent of the Owner, nor in time of war, but in a manner to be prescribed by law.

AMENDMENT IV

The right of the people to be secure in their persons, houses, papers, and effects, against unreasonable searches and seizures, shall not be violated, and no Warrants shall issue, but upon probable cause, supported by Oath or affirmation, and particularly describing the place to be searched, and the persons or things to be seized.

AMENDMENT V

No person shall be held to answer for a capital, or otherwise infamous crime, unless on a presentment or indictment of a Grand Jury, except in cases arising in the land or naval forces, or in the Militia, when in actual service in time of War or public danger; nor shall any person be subject for the same offence to be twice put in jeopardy of life or limb; nor shall be compelled in any criminal case to be a witness against himself, nor be deprived of life, liberty, or property, without due process of law; nor shall private property be taken for public use, without just compensation.

AMENDMENT VI

In all criminal prosecutions, the accused shall enjoy the right to a speedy and public trial, by an impartial jury of the State and district wherein the crime shall have been committed, which district shall have been previously ascertained by law, and to be informed of the nature and cause of the accusation; to be confronted with the witnesses against him; to have compulsory process for obtaining witnesses in his favor, and to have the Assistance of Counsel for his defence.

AMENDMENT VII

In Suits at common law, where the value in controversy shall exceed twenty dollars, the right of trial by jury shall be preserved, and no fact tried by a jury, shall be otherwise re-examined in any Court of the United States, than according to the rules of the common law.

AMENDMENT VIII

Excessive bail shall not be required, nor excessive fines imposed, nor cruel and unusual punishments inflicted.

AMENDMENT IX

The enumeration in the Constitution, of certain rights, shall not be construed to deny or disparage others retained by the people.

AMENDMENT X

The powers not delegated to the United States by the Constitution, nor prohibited by it to the States, are reserved to the States respectively, or to the people.

AMENDMENT XI

The Judicial power of the United States shall not be construed to extend to any suit in law or equity, commenced or prosecuted against one on the United States by Citizens of another State, or by Citizens or Subjects of any Foreign State.

AMENDMENT XII

The Electors shall meet in their respective states and vote by ballot for President and Vice-President, one of whom, at least, shall not be an inhabitant of the same state with themselves; they shall name in their ballots the person voted for as President, and in distinct ballots the person voted for as Vice-President, and they shall make distinct lists of all persons voted for as President, and of all persons voted for as Vice-President, and of the number of votes for each, which lists they shall sign and certify, and transmit sealed to the seat of the government of the United States, directed to the President of the Senate;—The President of the Senate shall, in the presence of the Senate and House of Representatives, open all the certificates and the votes shall then be counted;—The person having the greatest Number of votes for President, shall be the President, if such number be a majority of the whole number of Electors appointed; and if no person have such majority, then from the persons having the highest numbers not exceeding three on the list of those voted for as President, the House of Representatives shall choose immediately, by ballot, the President. But in choosing the President, the votes shall be taken by states, the representation from each state having one vote; a quorum for this purpose shall consist of a member or members from two-thirds of the states, and a majority of all the states shall be necessary to a choice. And if the House of Representatives shall not choose a President whenever the right of choice shall devolve upon them, before the fourth day of March next following, then the Vice-President shall act as President, as in the case of the death or other constitutional disability of the President—The person having the greatest number of votes as Vice-President, shall be the Vice-President, if such number be a majority of the whole number of Electors appointed, and if no person have a majority, then from the two highest numbers on the list, the Senate shall choose the Vice-President; a quorum for the purpose shall consist of two-thirds of the whole number of Senators, and a majority of the whole number shall be necessary to a choice. But no person constitutionally ineligible to the office of President shall be eligible to that of Vice President of the United States.

AMENDMENT XIII

SECTION. 1. Neither slavery nor involuntary servitude, except as a punishment for crime whereof the party shall have been duly convicted, shall exist within the United States, or any place subject to their jurisdiction.

SECTION. 2. Congress shall have power to enforce this article by appropriate legislation.

AMENDMENT XIV

SECTION. 1. All persons born or naturalized in the United States and subject to the jurisdiction thereof, are citizens of the United States and of the State wherein they reside. No State shall make or enforce any law which shall abridge the privileges or immunities of citizens of the United States; nor shall any State deprive any person of life, liberty, or property, without due process of law; nor deny to any person within its jurisdiction the equal protection of the laws.

SECTION. 2. Representatives shall be apportioned among the several States according to their respective numbers, counting the whole number of persons in each State, excluding Indians not taxed. But when the right to vote at any election for the choice of electors for President and Vice President of the United States, Representatives in Congress, the Executive and Judicial officers of a State, or the members of the Legislature thereof, is denied to any of the male inhabitants of such State, being twenty-one years of age, and citizens of the United States, or in any way abridged, except for participation in rebellion, or other crime, the basis of representation therein shall be reduced in the proportion which the number of such male citizens shall bear to the whole number of male citizens twenty one years of age in such State.

SECTION. 3. No person shall be a Senator or Representative in Congress, or elector of President and Vice President, or hold any office, civil or military, under the United States, or under any State, who, having previously taken an oath, as a member of Congress, or as an officer of the United States, or as a member of any State legislature, or as an executive or judicial officer of any State, to support the Constitution of the United States, shall have engaged in insurrection or rebellion against the same, or given aid or comfort to the enemies thereof. But Congress may by a vote of two-thirds of each House, remove such disability.

SECTION. 4. The validity of the public debt of the United States, authorized by law, including debts incurred for payment of pensions and bounties for services in suppressing insurrection or rebellion, shall not be questioned. But neither the United States nor any State shall assume or pay any debt or obligation incurred in aid of insurrection or rebellion against the United States, or any claim for the loss or emancipation of any slave; but all such debts, obligations and claims shall be held illegal and void.

SECTION. 5. The Congress shall have power to enforce, by appropriate legislation, the provisions of this article.

AMENDMENT XV
SECTION. 1. The right of citizens of the United States to vote shall not be denied or abridged by the United States or by any State on account of race, color, or previous condition of servitude.

SECTION. 2. The Congress shall have power to enforce this article by appropriate legislation.

AMENDMENT XVI
The Congress shall have power to lay and collect taxes on incomes, from whatever source derived, without apportionment among the several States, and without regard to any census or enumeration.

AMENDMENT XVII

The Senate of the United States shall be composed of two Senators from each State, elected by the people thereof, for six years; and each Senator shall have one vote. The electors in each State shall have the qualifications requisite for electors of the most numerous branch of the State legislatures. When vacancies happen in the representation of any State in the Senate, the executive authority of such State shall issue writs of election to fill such vacancies: Provided, That the legislature of any State may empower the executive thereof to make temporary appointments until the people fill the vacancies by election as the legislature may direct. This amendment shall not be so construed as to affect the election or term of any Senator chosen before it becomes valid as part of the Constitution.

AMENDMENT XVIII

SECTION. 1. After one year from the ratification of this article the manufacture, sale, or transportation of intoxicating liquors within, the importation thereof into, or the exportation thereof from the United States and all territory subject to the jurisdiction thereof for beverage purposes is hereby prohibited.

SECTION. 2. The Congress and the several States shall have concurrent power to enforce this article by appropriate legislation.

SECTION. 3. This article shall be inoperative unless it shall have been ratified as an amendment to the Constitution by the legislatures of the several States, as provided in the Constitution, within seven years from the date of the submission hereof to the States by the Congress.

AMENDMENT XIX

The right of citizens of the United States to vote shall not be denied or abridged by the United States or by any State on account of sex.

Congress shall have power to enforce this article by appropriate legislation.

AMENDMENT XX

SECTION. 1. The terms of the President and Vice President shall end at noon on the 20th day of January, and the terms of Senators and Representatives at noon on the 3d day of January, of the years in which such terms would have ended if this article had not been ratified; and the terms of their successors shall then begin.

SECTION. 2. The Congress shall assemble at least once in every year, and such meeting shall begin at noon on the 3d day of January, unless they shall by law appoint a different day.

SECTION. 3. If, at the time fixed for the beginning of the term of the President, the President elect shall have died, the Vice-President elect shall become President. If a President shall not have been chosen before the time fixed for the beginning of his term, or if the President elect shall have failed to qualify, then the Vice President elect shall act as President until a President shall have qualified; and the Congress may by law provide for the case wherein neither a President elect nor a Vice President elect shall have qualified, declaring who shall then act as President, or the manner in which one who is to act shall be selected, and such person shall act accordingly until a President or Vice President shall have qualified.

SECTION. 4. The Congress may by law provide for the case of the death of any of the persons from whom the House of Representatives may choose a President whenever the right of choice shall have devolved upon them, and for the case of the death of any of the persons from whom the Senate may choose a Vice President whenever the right of choice shall have devolved upon them.

SECTION. 5. Sections 1 and 2 shall take effect on the 15th day of October following the ratification of this article.

SECTION. 6. This article shall be inoperative unless it shall have been ratified as an amendment to the Constitution by the legislatures of three-fourths of the several States within seven years from the date of its submission.

AMENDMENT XXI

SECTION. 1. The eighteenth article of amendment to the Constitution of the United States is hereby repealed.

SECTION. 2. The transportation or importation into any State, Territory, or possession of the United States for delivery or use therein of intoxicating liquors, in violation of the laws thereof, is hereby prohibited.

SECTION. 3. This article shall be inoperative unless it shall have been ratified as an amendment to the Constitution by conventions in the several States, as provided in the Constitution, within seven years from the date of the submission hereof to the States by the Congress.

AMENDMENT XXII

SECTION. 1. No person shall be elected to the office of the President more than twice, and no person who has held the office of President, or acted as President, for more than two years of a term to which some other person was elected President shall be elected to the office of the President more than once. But this Article shall not apply to any person holding the office of President, when this Article was proposed by the Congress, and shall not prevent any person who may be holding the office of President, or acting as President, during the term within which this Article becomes operative from holding the office of President or acting as President during the remainder of such term.

SECTION. 2. This article shall be inoperative unless it shall have been ratified as an amendment to the Constitution by the legislatures of three-fourths of the several States within seven years from the date of its submission to the States by the Congress.

AMENDMENT XXIII

SECTION. 1. The District constituting the seat of Government of the United States shall appoint in such manner as the Congress may direct: A number of electors of President and Vice President equal to the whole number of Senators and Representatives in Congress to which the District would be entitled if it were a State, but in no event more than the least populous State; they shall be in addition to those appointed by the States, but they shall be considered, for the purposes of the election of President and Vice President, to be electors appointed by a State; and they shall meet in the District and perform such duties as provided by the twelfth article of amendment.

SECTION. 2. The Congress shall have power to enforce this article by appropriate legislation.

AMENDMENT XXIV

SECTION. 1. The right of citizens of the United States to vote in any primary or other election for President or Vice President, for electors for President or Vice President, or for Senator or Representative in Congress, shall not be denied or abridged by the United States or any State by reason of failure to pay any poll tax or other tax.

SECTION. 2. The Congress shall have power to enforce this article by appropriate legislation.

AMENDMENT XXV

SECTION. 1. In case of the removal of the President from office or of his death or resignation, the Vice President shall become President.

SECTION. 2. Whenever there is a vacancy in the office of the Vice President, the President shall nominate a Vice President who shall take office upon confirmation by a majority vote of both Houses of Congress.

SECTION. 3. Whenever the President transmits to the President pro tempore of the Senate and the Speaker of the House of Representatives has written declaration that he is unable to discharge the powers and duties of his office, and until he transmits to them a written declaration to the contrary, such powers and duties shall be discharged by the Vice President as Acting President.

SECTION. 4. Whenever the Vice President and a majority of either the principal officers of the executive departments or of such other body as Congress may by law provide, transmit to the President pro tempore of the Senate and the Speaker of the House of Representatives their written declaration that the President is unable to discharge the powers and duties of his office, the Vice President shall immediately assume the powers and duties of the office as Acting President.

Thereafter, when the President transmits to the President pro tempore of the Senate and the Speaker of the House of Representatives his written declaration that no inability exists, he shall resume the powers and duties of his office unless the Vice President and a majority of either the principal officers of the executive department or of such other body as Congress may by law provide, transmit within four days to the President pro tempore of the Senate and the Speaker of the House of Representatives their written declaration that the President is unable to discharge the powers and duties of his office. Thereupon Congress shall decide the issue, assembling within forty-eight hours for that purpose if not in session. If the Congress, within twenty-one days after receipt of the latter written declaration, or, if Congress is not in session, within twenty-one days after Congress is required to assemble, determines by two-thirds vote of both Houses that the President is unable to discharge the powers and duties of his office, the Vice President shall continue to discharge the same as Acting President; otherwise, the President shall resume the powers and duties of his office.

AMENDMENT XXVI
SECTION. 1. The right of citizens of the United States, who are eighteen years of age or older, to vote shall not be denied or abridged by the United States or by any State on account of age.

SECTION. 2. The Congress shall have power to enforce this article by appropriate legislation.

AMENDMENT XXVII
No law varying the compensation for the services of the Senators and Representatives shall take effect, until an election of Representatives shall have intervened.

This text of the Constitution is a transcription of the document in its original form. For a transcription with hyperlinks that show how sections of the Constitution have been superseded by Amendment view the US Government Archives Constitution.

Selected Bibliography

The following books are important resources on the Founding Documents and the cultural heritage of the United States.

Adams, John, *John Adams: Revolutionary Writings 1775–1783*, Library of America; 1st edition (March 31, 2011)

Amar, Akhil Reed, *The Constitution and Criminal Procedure: First Principles*, Yale University Press (March 30, 1998)

Amar, Akhil Reed, *The Bill of Rights: Creation and Reconstruction*, Yale University Press (April 1, 2000)

Amar, Akhil Reed, *America's Constitution: A Biography*, Random House; 1st Edition (August 18, 2010)

Amar, Akhil Reed, *America's Unwritten Constitution: The Precedents and Principles We Live By*, Basic Books; Reprint edition (January 6, 2015)

Barnett, Randy, *Rights Retained by the People: The History and Meaning of the Ninth Amendment*, University Publishers Association (November 27, 1989)

Berkin, Carol, *A Brilliant Solution: Inventing the American Constitution*, Mariner Books; Reprint edition (October 20, 2003)

Bowenun, Catherine Drinker, *Miracle At Philadelphia: The Story of the Constitutional Convention May–September 1787*, Back Bay Books; 1st Edition (September 30, 1986)

Commission on the Bicentennial of the United States Constitution, *1791–1991, The Bill of Rights and Beyond* (1991)

Cogan, Neil H., Editor, *The Complete Bill of Rights*, Oxford University Press, Oxford (1997)

De Tocqueville, Alexis, *Democracy in America*, Penguin Classics (July 1, 2003)

Farber, Dan, *Retained by the People: The "Silent" Ninth Amendment and the Constitutional Rights Americans Don't Know They Have*, Basic Books; 1st Edition (May 1, 2007)

Farish, Leah, *The First Amendment: Freedom of Speech, Religion, and the Press*, Enslow Publishers (1998)

Fraden, Dennis, *The Signers: The Fifty-Six Stories Behind the Declaration of Independence*, Walker (2002)

Freedman, Russel, *In Defense of Liberty: The Story of America's Bill of Rights,* Holiday House (2003)

Friendly, Fred W., Elliott, Martha, *The Constitution, That Delicate Balance*, Random House, NY (1984)

Fritz, Jean, *Shh! We're Writing the Constitution*, Puffin Books; Reissue edition (December 29, 1997)

Harper, Timothy, *The Complete Idiot's Guide to the U.S. Constitution*, Alpha (October 2, 2007)

Hermalyn, Gary D., Ultan, Lloyd Editors, *The Signers of the Constitution*, Bronx County Historical Society, Bronx, NY (1987)

Hutchinson, David, *The Foundations of the Constitution*, University Books, Seacaucus, NJ (1975)

Jay, John, Madison, James, Hamilton, Alexander, edited by Benjamin Fletcher Wright *The Federalist Papers*, Barnes and Noble Books (1996)

Judson, Karen, *The Constitution of the United States: Its History, Bill of Rights, and Amendments*, Enslow (2013)

Ketcham, Ralph, Editor, *The Anti-Federalist Papers and the Constitutional Convention Debates*, New American Library (1986)

Levy, Leonard W., *Origins of the Bill of Rights*, Yale University Press (1999)

Madison, James, *James Madison: Writings: 1772–1836*, Library of America (August 30, 1999)

Maier, Pauline, *American Scripture, Making the Declaration of Independence*, Vintage Books, New York (1997)

Maier Pauline, *Ratification: The People Debate The Constitution*, Simon and Schuster, New York (2011)

McWhirter, Darien, *Freedom of Speech, Press, and Assembly*, Oryx (1994)

Monk, Linda R., *The Words We Live By*, Hyperion, New York, NY (2003)

Monk, Linda R., *The Words We Live By: Your Annotated Guide to the Constitution*, Hachette Books (August 18, 2010)

Natelson, Robert G., *The Original Constitution: What it Actually Said and Meant*, 2nd Edition, Create Space Independent Publishing Platform (May 17, 2010)

Paine, Thomas, *Common Sense* (Dover Thrift Editions), Dover Publications (April 22, 1997)

Palmer, Kris, Editor, *Constitutional Amendments, 1789 to the Present*, Gale Group, Inc., Farmington Hills, MI (2000)

Ritchie, Donald A., *Our Constitution*, Oxford University Press, Oxford, New York (2006)

Signer, Michael, *Becoming Madison: The Extraordinary Origins of the Least Likely Founding Father*, Public Affairs (2015)

Skousen, W. Cleon, *The 5000 Year Leap*, National Center for Constitutional Studies (January 1, 2007)

St. John, Jeffrey, *Forge of Union, Anvil of Liberty*, Jameson Books Inc.; First edition (June 1992)

St. John, Jeffrey, *Constitutional Journal*, Jameson Books Inc., 1st Edition (June 1, 1987)

Stewart, David O., *The Summer of 1787: The Men Who Invented the Constitution*, Simon and Schuster (2007)

Wood, Gordon S., *Revolutionary Characters: What Made the Founders Different*, Penguin Books, Reprint Edition (May 18, 2006)